The United States Supreme Court

A political and legal analysis

Robert J. McKeever

MANCHESTER UNIVERSITY PRESS
Manchester and New York

distributed exclusively in the USA by St. Martin's Press

Published by Manchester University Press
Oxford Road, Manchester M13 9NR, UK
and Room 400, 175 Fifth Avenue, New York, NY 10010, USA

Distributed exclusively in the USA
by St. Martin's Press, Inc., 175 Fifth Avenue, New York
NY 10010, USA

British Library Cataloguing-in-Publication Data

A catalogue record for this book is available from the British Library

Library of Congress Cataloguing-in-Publication Data applied for

ISBN   0 7190 4081 7 *hardback*
        0 7190 4082 5 *paperback*

First published 1997

01 00 99 98 97   10 9 8 7 6 5 4 3 2 1

Photoset in Ehrhardt
by Northern Phototypesetting Co. Ltd., Bolton
Printed in Great Britain
by Biddles Ltd, Guildford and King's Lynn

Contents

Figures

Tables

Preface

When I was first asked to write an introductory level book on the United States Supreme Court, I must confess to having had reservations. It was not that I had any doubts about the need for new students of American politics to understand the role played by the Court: after all, time has only added credence to Alexis de Tocqueville's famous perception in the 1830s that 'scarcely any political question arises in the United State that is not resolved, sooner or later, into a judicial question'. But less well-known is de Tocqueville's apprehension that he might not be able to render his study of the American judiciary interesting to non-lawyers. As he put it:

> But how can one make the political action of American tribunals understandable without entering into some technical details of their constitution and procedures? And how can one plunge into these arid details of a naturally arid subject, without rebuffing the reader's curiosity? How can one remain clear and still be brief?
>
> I don't flatter myself that I have avoided these different perils. Lay readers will find me too lengthy, and lawyers too brief. But that is an inevitable disadvantage of my whole subject, and of this specialised part of it in particular.

Amen to all that.

Nevertheless, the aim of this book is to overcome these difficulties and to convince students and teachers of American politics that the Supreme Court is every bit as important, accessible and fascinating a topic of study as the Congress or the presidency. Certainly the problems posed by confronting readers with unfamiliar legal terminology and procedure are real, but they are not insurmountable. My own undergraduates who have studied the Court with me have proved that.

In fact, any student reading about the Court or reading its actual Opinions soon grasps the fact that while law and judicial procedure provide the framework for Supreme Court decisions, politics is often central to their substance. One cannot understand the nature and role of the Supreme Court, therefore, without an appreciation of its dual nature as a political and legal body. But it is precisely this blend of politics and law which makes the United States Supreme Court a unique and stimulating object of study.

No one, I am sure, needs convincing that racial equality, abortion or freedom of the press are highly political issues in the United States. Nor is there any doubt that the Supreme Court has been a central player in the policy-making process on these matters. But the real fun of studying the Court begins with the realisation that the Justices are obliged to approach these policy issues in a manner quite different from that of the President or members of Congress. And the distinctively *judicial* approach to policy-making draws upon not merely legal reasoning, but large doses of political philosophy, history and social morality. To study the Supreme Court, then, is to study the interplay of American politics, law and culture when they meet in the federal court-room.

With these perspectives in mind, I have set out the structure of the book as follows. Chapter One aims to win the reader's interest in the most direct fashion: it examines some of the fascinating policy issues that are central to the Court by examining its contemporary agenda. It analyses the Court's major decisions on controversial issues such as race, abortion, capital punishment and gay rights. At the same time, it addresses the vital underlying question of how the Court's agenda is broadly determined at any given point in its history. I have not attempted to be comprehensive in my coverage of the Court's contemporary agenda, since that would require a separate book in itself; and there are already several useful texts which do just that. I hope, however, that the issues I do analyse will give the reader a good idea of the character of the Court's contemporary agenda, as well as its genesis and import for modern American government.

Chapter Two then takes a step back and investigates how the framers of the Constitution envisaged the nature and the role of the Supreme Court, and how and why these have evolved.

Chapter Three takes up the specifically judicial and legal basics of the Court's structure and processes and looks at the rules and procedures which govern the Justices' work. If these are indeed, as de Tocqueville would have it, the most 'arid' aspects of the Supreme Court, they are nonetheless vital to an understanding of the special way in which the Court operates.

Chapter Four examines the key concept of judicial review, the source of the Court's power. In particular, the focus is on the ways in which political considerations have become increasingly prominent in constitutional interpretation in the twentieth century and on why this development is problematic for the Court's role.

Chapter Five analyses one of the most controversial features of the contemporary Supreme Court, the process of appointing new Justices. The Robert Bork and Clarence Thomas nominations were merely the tip of a political iceberg and so we examine the the the politicisation of the appointment process.

Chapters Six and Seven take up perhaps the most important questions of all: how powerful is the Court and what is its role in American government and politics today?

Each chapter is designed to be self-contained so that, as far as possible, readers can dip into the book according to their needs and interests. This inevitably involves a certain amount of repetition, but hopefully not so much that it proves irksome for those who choose to read the book whole.

Any book which seeks to introduce readers to a new field of study has the obligation to inform accurately and explain coherently. Naturally, I hope I have fulfilled these demands, at least to the point where both teachers and students will find this book useful. I hope also, however, to have conveyed something of my own enthusiasm for the subject. For it is my abiding conviction that there is no better way to join the American debate over key issues such as abortion and race, and key concepts such as liberty and equality, than to study the Supreme Court.

Acknowledgments

A book such as this, generated from many years of study, teaching and scholarship, reflects the influence of numerous individuals and institutions. The cohorts of students who have taken my course on the Court at Reading have both alerted me to some of the problems involved in teaching it and also indicated some of the solutions. Members of the American Politics Group of the Political Studies Association always provide a congenial forum for the scrutiny of one's ideas on judicial politics, particularly Richard Hodder-Williams of Bristol University, a fellow Court enthusiast and sharp, but always fair critic.

Most academic writers owe a good deal to libraries. And studying the United States Supreme Court from the UK would have been so much more difficult without the facilities afforded by the Institute of Advanced Legal Studies in London.

I should also like to thank Richard Purslow who suggested this book to me when he was Politics Editor at Manchester University Press and, as always, was enthusiastic and supportive. Thanks too to Nicola Viinikka, who took over from Richard and cheerfully saw it through to completion.

Finally my greatest thanks must go to Richard Maidment, of the Open University. I first encountered Richard in his capacity as my Ph.D. supervisor at Keele University. Since overseeing my first real attempt at Supreme Court scholarship, he has become both mentor and good friend, and this book bears his imprint in many ways.

Any errors and weaknesses, alas, are all mine.

This book is for Catherine

One—The Court's contemporary agenda

For many people, the most important and interesting aspect of the Supreme Court is the actual decisions the Justices take on the great issues and controversies of the day. We begin, therefore, by an examination of the Court's contemporary agenda: what are the great questions of public policy that come before the Court today and how have the Justices tried to resolve them? We also look at the main factors which drive the Court's agenda-setting process.

Politics and the legal agenda

One of the most frequently quoted statements about the Supreme Court's agenda is the observation by Alexis de Tocqueville in the 1830s that 'scarcely any political question arises in the United States that is not resolved, sooner or later, into a judicial question'. Although there is a significant element of exaggeration here, de Tocqueville brilliantly perceived the most critical aspect of the Court's agenda: that the major issues which come before the Justices have their origins in the political arena, not the law.

De Tocqueville's observation does need to be qualified, however. For the Court never attempts to deal with all the political questions that arise in any historical era. Rather the Justices select among those questions and choose only a relatively small number of them for judicial consideration. In short, throughout American history, the Supreme Court's agenda has been determined by the nation's political agenda, as filtered by the Justices' discretionary powers.

This means, of course, that the major issues before the Court have varied over time, depending on the shifting focus of American politics. Thus, in the early decades of the new Constitution, the Court's most significant cases concerned such fundamental issues as federalism: that is, the allocation of powers between the States and the new federal (or national) government. There were also many important cases concerning the power of both the States and the new national government to regulate business activity and property rights.

That these issues should have preoccupied the Court at that time is not surprising. The Constitution was new and it was by no means clear exactly how much power the new federal government would wield. The American people wanted a government that worked better than the old one, but they did not want to give too much power to a distant national government in Washington. On the economic front, there were those who wanted the government actively to promote national commerce, while others feared the power of an alliance between the national government and the economic elite. These tensions quickly fuelled political controversy and almost inevitably found their way into the Supreme Court.

By the mid-nineteenth century, however, much of the heat had gone out of these controversies and the Court's agenda reflected that. Instead, the nation's politics was becoming increasingly obsessed with the issue of slavery. Sure enough, the 1840s saw the first slavery cases come before the Supreme Court. These culminated in the infamous Dred Scott case in 1857, when the Court strongly upheld slaveholders' rights, thus helping to precipitate the Civil War that broke out in 1861 (see Chapter Three).

After the Civil War, the political agenda changed again, as new issues arose in the wake of the rapid industrialisation that was sweeping the country. Among other things, the Court decided cases involving the rights of trade unions, the power of the government to regulate monopoly corporations and the constitutionality of a federal income tax. These economic conflicts came to a head in the 1930s as a result of the Great Depression. This economic and social catastrophe persuaded the government in Washington to take on unprecedented powers and responsibilities for the nation's well-being. There were, however, those who strongly objected to this expansion and they took their cause to the Supreme Court.

Once the Great Depression was over and the political controversies which it had generated had been settled, the Supreme Court turned its attention to a new batch of issues that were forcing their way onto the nation's political agenda. The most important of these arose from the civil rights movement of the post-World War II decades, which demanded equal rights for black Americans. In subsequent years, however, other disadvantaged groups took their cue from the civil rights movement and campaigned for equal or fairer treatment in law. One result of this was that over the last twenty-five years, groups such as women, homosexuals and environmentalists have filed numerous cases in the Supreme Court.

Table 1.1 The Court's agenda: selected periods, number of cases decided (% of total cases)

Issues	1933–37	1953–57	1983–87
Substantive rights	9	38	80
(e.g. abortion, free speech)	(1.2%)	(7.7%)	(10.7%)
Equality	11	25	124
(e.g. race, gender discrimination)	(1.4%)	(5.1%)	(16.6%)
Due process	41	84	222
(e.g. rights of accused, fair trial)	(5.2%)	(17.1%)	(29.6%)
US economic regulation	220	162	133
	(27.8%)	(33.0%)	(17.8%)
State economic regulation	79	10	8
	(10.1%)	(2.0%)	(1.1%)
Taxation	139	41	24
	(17.8%)	(8.4%)	(3.2%)

Source: Data adapted from L. Epstein, J. Segal, H. Spaeth and T. Walker, *The Supreme Court Compendium: Data, Decisions and Developments*, Washington, D.C., 1994, pp. 74–5.

Table 1.1 gives some detailed illustrations of the change in the Court's agenda from the 1930s through to the 1980s. In the 1930s the Court wrestled with the question of how much government regulation of private economic enterprise could be permitted, without violating individual economic liberties that were guaranteed by the Constitution. Thus, in the period 1933–37, cases involving state and federal government regulation of the economy and taxation accounted for over half of the Court's cases. Gradually, however, the prominence of these issues faded, although they did not disappear altogether, and in the period 1983–87 they accounted for less than a quarter of all cases.

Over the same period, however, cases involving non-economic civil rights and liberties came to the fore, with the Court tackling such issues as race and gender equality and the rights of criminals. Whereas these had barely featured on the Court's docket in the 1930s, they constituted over half of its cases by the 1980s.

Even this cursory glance over American history makes it clear that the Court's agenda in these different periods reflects the social and political conflicts of the day. The next step in understanding the Court's agenda, therefore, is to examine why these major political issues tend to be transformed into legal disputes and end up before the highest court in the land. So before we look in detail at the substance of the Court's contemporary agenda, it is necessary to address two broad questions. First, why do people take their political causes to the Supreme Court? And second, why do the Justices agree to adjudicate some of these causes, but reject others?

Political causes and the Supreme Court

It is important to be clear at the outset why individuals or groups decide to take their cause to the judiciary and eventually to the Supreme Court. And the first major point to grasp is that for most of its history, the Court has functioned as the last resort of those who have been unsuccessful in the political arena. In fact, as we shall see in Chapter Two, the very origins of the Supreme Court's power of judicial review lie partly in the electoral defeat of the Federalists in the elections of 1800. The Federalists feared the radicalism of the incoming Jeffersonian Republicans, but they hoped that, by packing the Court with staunch Federalists, they would be able to curb the worst excesses that might lie ahead.

Similarly, when industrialisation brought increasingly successful demands by voters for social and economic regulation on behalf of the lower classes, property owners and businesspeople sought the support of unelected judges in resisting such demands. Thus, for those who are in the electoral minority, the Supreme Court offers a last chance of salvation. To put it another way, the Supreme Court can transform political losers into constitutional winners.

Judicial review trumps legislation

The Supreme Court can do this because it possesses the power of *judicial review* (see Chapters Two and Four). This is the authority to declare any law or governmental action invalid, because the Justices of the Supreme Court believe that it violates one or more clauses of the Constitution. As the Constitution is the highest law of the land, a Supreme Court decision declaring a congressional or state statute unconstitutional is a 'trump card' in American politics. The only way it can be overcome outside the Court is by the extremely complex and difficult process of constitutional amendment.

This brings us to a second basic point about taking a political cause to the Supreme Court: something more than a mere political cause is required. Would-be litigants must present their political cause in the form of a constitutional claim. In other words, the civil rights movement of the 1950s could not go before the Court armed only with the argument that racial equality would be a good thing both for blacks and American society in general. For that is essentially a political argument.

Rather the movement had to identify a clause in the Constitution which *required* state legislatures to practise racial equality, regardless of its political benefits. In this instance it was relatively easy, because the Fourteenth Amendment to the Constitution (1868) was passed after the Civil War to stop the States from denying any citizen, and especially freed slaves, 'the equal protection of the laws'.

At first glance, the need to identify a clause in the Constitution which supports a political cause appears to be a major obstacle. After all, the Constitution is a brief document, mostly couched in general terms. It therefore contains very few specific references to political rights. This vagueness and generality has, however, been turned to the advantage of those seeking redress under the Constitution. For if it so inclined, the Court can take a broad, vague phrase and interpret it to apply to a specific situation. It can even change the very meaning of the phrase, so that it can be applied to new rights.

The Due Process clause of the Fourteenth Amendment is an outstanding case in point. It is framed in terms of legal procedure: 'nor shall any State deprive any person of life, liberty, or property, without due process of law'. Initially, this was taken to mean that individuals *could* be deprived of life, liberty or property, provided this was done according to established legal procedures. The essence of procedural Due Process, then, is the right to a fair hearing before the government may deprive a person of property or liberty.

In the late nineteenth century, however, the Court began to read the Due Process clause to contain substantive rights, as well as procedural rights. In other words, it held that certain unspecified liberty or property rights could never be taken away by government, even if it followed correct procedures.

Early on, for example, this new so-called 'substantive due process' was held to protect liberty of contract and hence to bar most forms of government intervention in labour relations. In practice and effect, it was used to support employers in their industrial disputes with their employees. It is important to stress that there is no reference to 'liberty of contract' in the Constitution. Rather, the Supreme Court effectively read it into the Constitution because it believed that liberty of contract was so fundamental to any meaningful definition of the Fourteenth Amendment's broad reference to liberty, that it must be placed beyond the reach of government.

By the late 1930s, however, that understanding of liberty in the Due Process clause had been abandoned. In effect, absolute liberty of contract had lost its place at the top of the hierarchy of 'fundamental values' protected by substantive due process. But in the 1960s a new form of substantive due process emerged which supported such liberties as the right to use contraceptives or to terminate a pregnancy by abortion. In other words, an economic concept of substantive due process rights had given way to one based upon 'privacy' and rights to personal autonomy.

Just as there is no mention of 'liberty of contract' in the Constitution, you will look in vain for any reference to 'privacy' there. Substantive due process rights, then, depend for their existence upon the Justices of the Supreme Court deeming them fundamental to a meaningful definition of individual liberty. And such notions of individual liberty clearly vary between different historical eras and, indeed, between different Supreme Court Justices within the same era.

In short, the definition of constitutional terms and liberties is always subject to change and expansion (or, indeed, contraction), if the Justices have a mind to do so. Individuals and groups are therefore encouraged to turn to the Court, even where past interpretation of the Constitution is not on their side. At the very least, then, the Supreme Court can offer hope where the political process offers none. A new era, new ways of thinking and, of course, new Supreme Court Justices always bring the possibility of new interpretations of constitutional terms.

Having noted that the Court has historically offered hope to *political* or *electoral minorities*, that is, those who have failed to attain their goals through elections and legislation, it is important not to confuse this with judicial support for *permanent minorities*, such as African-Americans.

The situation of electoral minorities on the one hand and permanent minorities on the other are quite different. An electoral minority can always take steps to join with other groups and make itself into an electoral majority. Permanent minorities which are feared or despised by the majority, however, have little or no such possibility available to them: they are simply not welcomed as coalition partners.

Nevertheless, despite the far greater weakness of permanent minorities in the political process, the Court throughout most of its history has been the last refuge of electoral minorities. Some sixty years ago, however, the Court began a conscious switch which led it to focus more on the rights of permanent minorities than those of political minorites pure and simple. And this switch provides one of the most important keys to understanding the Supreme Court's contemporary agenda.

The Court and permanent minorities: Justice Stone's Footnote Four

In 1937 the Court finally lost its battle with government to preserve a traditional concept of economic and property rights largely free from government regulation. In political terms, it thereby ceased to be a reactionary institution defending the economic rights of the wealthy minority against the demands of the electoral majority for greater economic justice. However, in abandoning its role as the last governmental champion of *laissez-faire* economics, the Court left itself without an agenda.

Yet almost immediately the Court sowed the seeds of a new one. In 1938, in the case of *US v. Carolene Products*, Justice Harlan Fiske Stone stated the new judicial orthodoxy on economic matters, arguing that the Court must show deference to Congress and apply a strong presumption of constitutionality when reviewing regulations of commerce. In an aside that became famous as 'Footnote Four', however, Stone raised the possibility that such deference might not be appropriate, and a 'more searching judicial inquiry' may be required, when statutes seemed aimed at racial, religious and 'discrete and insular minorities'. Stone's rationale was that such minority groups may be subject to enduring and immutable majority prejudice, with the result that the ordinary democratic political processes might not protect their rights. In other words, Stone was suggesting that the Court become the champion of those permanent minorities who were always liable to lose out in the political arena.

Stone's Footnote Four is a clear illustration of the way in which the Court can define its own agenda. There is nothing in the Constitution or in the theory of judicial review which suggests that economic issues should be treated differently from social issues, or that 'insular minorities' merit different judicial treatment from economic minorities. So when the Court decided to make Footnote Four the basis of its modern agenda, it was essentially an act of judicial will.

Of course, the Court's great decisions on the civil rights of black Americans only began to flow once these issues had emerged onto the nation's political agenda. The landmark school desegregation case of *Brown v. Board of Education* (1954) may have given new impetus to the civil rights movement, but the issue of racial equality was already on its way to political prominence by then. Thus *Brown* and other cases serve to underline the basic point that getting an issue onto the Court's agenda requires both that it is a prominent or emerging issue on the nation's political agenda and that the Court feels ready to address it.

The Court's discretionary power

It is worth noting at this point that the rules governing Supreme Court procedures leave the Justices almost entirely free to take or reject cases at will. This was not always so, but Congress has gradually eliminated the Court's obligation to take certain kinds of cases (see Chapter Three). Thus, while the Court is regularly petitioned to hear around 5,000 cases or more a year, it usually accepts only between 100 and 150. In other words, the Court accepts only around 2 or 3 per cent of cases filed with it.

Clearly, therefore, the few cases which are accepted must have certain special characteristics. Some of these are quasi-technical. For example, the Court will usually deem it necessary to take a case involving an issue which has been decided differently in different lower courts. This is essentially a matter of providing an authoritative and consistent ruling for all lower courts to follow.

Another factor which weighs heavily with the Justices is when the appeal is brought by the Solicitor General of the United States. Because the Justices have great respect for the Solicitor General and know that he will usually only bring serious and important cases to them, they accept between 75 and 90 per cent of the appeals from this source.[1]

Ultimately, however, the main reason the Justices agree to hear an appeal is the sheer importance of the issue involved. Perhaps a case has unique importance, as when the Court took *US v. Nixon* (1974) to determine whether President Nixon was obliged to hand over the White House tapes to the Special Prosecutor investigating the Watergate affair.

Usually, however, the Court will take a case because it involves an issue which the Justices recognise as one of great social significance. As we have seen, exactly what these issues are will vary from one era to the next, but in the contemporary period it is cases involving equality and personal non-economic liberties. It is also important to remember, however, that these issues must be linked to clauses in the Constitution. As Table 1.2 indicates, this leads to a situation in which the Court is highly receptive to claims which invoke some clauses rather than others.

Table 1.2 Most litigated constitutional provisions

Court	Constitutional provision	Number of cases
Warren Court	Equal Protection clause, 14th Am.	127
(1953–69)	Due Process clause, 14th Am.	125
	Freedom of speech/press/assembly, 1st Am.	74
Burger Court	Due Process clause, 14th Am.	214
(1969–86)	Equal Protection clause, 14th Am.	185
	Freedom of speech/press/assembly, 1st Am.	168
Rehnquist Court	Freedom of speech/press/assembly, 1st Am.	61
(1986–92)	Due Process clause, 14th Am.	56
	Case or controversy, Article III	34

Source: Data adapted from Epstein et al., The Supreme Court Compendium, pp. 555–6.

The Court's Modern Agenda

It did not take long for Justice Stone's concept of heightened protection for insular minorities to command a majority on the Court. For example, in 1940 Stone had been the lone dissenter in *Minersville School District v. Gobitis*, where the Court turned down a claim by Jehovah's Witnesses that the compulsory flag salute in schools violated their religious freedom under the First Amendment.

Just three years later, however, that decision was reversed in *West Virginia Board of Education v. Barnette*. In the intervening period, the United States had entered World War II, with an accompanying upsurge in patriotism. This had expressed itself in numerous physical attacks upon Jehovah's Witnesses who continued to refuse to pledge allegiance to the flag. If nothing else, such majoritarian prejudice clearly stamped Jehovah's Witnesses as an insular religious minority in need of protection and the Court now responded in line with Footnote Four.

Racial segregation

Undoubtedly the group that was to benefit most from the Court's new agenda of protection for the rights of insular minorities was black Americans. The Thirteenth, Fourteenth and Fifteenth Amendments to the Constitution had been designed to ensure that the slaves freed as a result of the Civil War would have the same legal and political rights as other Americans. Yet state legislatures had repeatedly denied blacks these rights and all too often, the Supreme Court had turned a blind eye to such constitutional violations.

Most infamous of all was the decision in *Plessy v. Ferguson* (1896), where the Court ruled that the segregation of railroad cars did not violate the Equal Protection clause of the Fourteenth Amendment. The Court reasoned that 'separate but equal' facilities did not imply any inferiority of blacks, even if they chose to see it that way! As a result of *Plessy*, the Court effectively gave constitutional blessing to all racially segregated facilities, which commonly included schools, restaurants, hotels, parks and even cemeteries.

Segregation was by no means the whole story of racial discrimination, however. In the South in particular, blacks were prevented from exercising their Fifteenth Amendment right to vote by a variety of devices. White election officials, for example, employed literacy tests which required would-be voters to demonstrate their fitness to vote by, say, reading and explaining a clause of the state constitution. Needless to say, the vast majority of those who were deemed to have failed the test were blacks.

Yet another discriminatory device was the 'white primary', employed in Texas. Like most Southern States, Texas politics was dominated by the Democratic Party and hence the winner of the Democratic primary election was guaranteed victory in the general election itself. Although the State could not constitutionally prevent blacks from voting in the general election, the Democratic primary was technically a private matter for the party. When the Texas Democrats duly excluded blacks from voting in its primary, the Court upheld the constitutionality of this blatantly discriminatory practice in *Grovey v. Townsend* (1935). The Court argued that the Fourteenth Amendment did not reach such 'private' discrimination.

Black Americans, then, were subjected to a vast array of legal, political and social forms of discrimination, which they could not rectify through normal political and electoral activity. The whole point about the subordination of blacks was that it was supported by the prejudices of the white majority who controlled the electoral and policy-making processes. Here, quite clearly, was the paradigm of a permanent minority whose rights and interests were not protected by the usual forms of majoritarian democratic politics.

Brown v. Board of Education (1954)   G of Dem

The Court did take some steps in the 1930s and 1940s that strengthened the civil rights of blacks. The Texas white primary was eventually struck down in *Smith v. Allwright* in 1944. And in *Missouri ex rel. Gaines v. Canada* (1938) and *McLaurin v. Oklahoma State Board of Regents* (1950) the Court at least began to insist that States make a genuine attempt to ensure the equality of separate education facilities.

It was, however, only with the great school desegregation decision in *Brown v. Board of Education* (1954) that the Supreme Court firmly embraced its new role as the champion of oppressed minorities. The case was the latest in a series brought by the National Association for the Advancement of Colored People (NAACP). The NAACP strategy was to build gradually to a situation where the Court struck down not just specific instances of racial segregation, but the very principle that underpinned them. That climax came in *Brown*.

The Court was confronted with the claim that the segregation of public elementary schools was unconstitutional under the Equal Protection clause of the Fourteenth Amendment, even if the different schools were equal in the tangible facilities provided. In other words, the notion of 'separate but equal' upheld in *Plessy* was constitutionally unacceptable. The Supreme Court agreed unanimously. Despite doubts as to whether the Fourteenth Amendment had been intended to prohibit racially segregated schools, the Justices decided that in the light of the importance of education today, such segregation amounted to a violation of the Equal Protection clause. Crucially, the Court held that 'separate but equal' facilites were, in fact, inherently and always unequal and hence the *Plessy* doctrine was overruled.

Although *Brown* dealt only with the issue of education, it clearly spelt the end of all forms of legalised racial segregation. And, sure enough, in the wake of *Brown*, the Court gradually ordered the desegregation of all public facilities. Although bitterly resented and resisted by many Americans, above all in the South, the *Brown* decision was hailed by many as one of the most just and noble in the entire history of the Court.

The legacy of *Brown*

Brown was obviously important for what it said about the constitutional rights of African-Americans. It was also important, however, for what it suggested about the role of the Supreme Court. As one author wrote:

> *Brown v. Board of Education* was an extraordinarily important case. It marked the first time since the New Deal that the Court deliberately intervened in the establishment of broad social policy. It achieved enough success that it came to be regarded as a kind of demonstration of the desirability and practicability of Court-made social policy. Without the confidence in a 'reforming' Court created by *Brown*, it is doubtful that the rest of the Warren Court years could have unfolded as they did.[2]

The Supreme Court, culture wars and social reform

In short, *Brown* was the catalyst for a new role for the Supreme Court: that of an agency for progressive social reform. In the twenty-five or so years following *Brown*, the Court took up a series of issues that it had either shied away from previously or that had never before been presented for judicial resolution.

This new phase of judicial activism differed in other important respects from earlier ones. Thus, whereas previous activist courts had been essentially conservative, the Warren Court (1953–69) was decidedly liberal. Moreover, earlier activist courts had been negative, in that their decisions usually obliged other branches of government to cease doing something. The Warren and early Burger Courts, however, were often positive, ordering government to do something it would not otherwise have done. The Court, for example, required government to provide lawyers for those who were accused of crimes but were too poor to pay for their own lawyers. It also required state governments to reapportion their legislatures and congressional districts to meet a strict standard of 'one person, one vote'. The Supreme Court, then, was employing the power of judicial review to place new affirmative responsibilities on government.

Brown was also a catalyst for the new activism in the sense that interest groups pursuing progressive social reform modelled their own litigation strategies on that employed by the NAACP. At the very least, they now perceived constitutional litigation as a viable and, perhaps, the best means of influencing public policy. Interest groups were thus an important factor in turning *Brown* from a unique episode in the Court's history into a blueprint for judicial action on a broad range of issues.

The Justices' own activist inclinations and the exhortations of interest groups were both fed, of course, by the widespread spirit of unconventional thought which shook American politics and culture in the 1960s and 1970s. In those two decades, the old consensus on cultural values was split asunder. Radical youth, black militants, feminists, environmentalists and gays and lesbians all challenged fundamental precepts of traditional American culture, including the great trilogy of family, country and God. Amongst other things, these radicals demanded more government action to make the races genuinely equal; defied conventional sexual morality; opposed the war in Vietnam; supported a more liberal system of criminal justice; questioned the validity of the Protestant work ethic and capitalist values generally; and demanded a fundamental change in gender relations.

These 'culture wars' had clear implications for public policy on a wide array of issues. For if women were to be treated as the equal of men, or individuals to be given much greater autonomy over their personal lives, then quite simply many state and federal laws would have to be changed. And urged on by interest groups, the Supreme Court decided that it had an important role to play in the process of reform. Let us now examine the reforming decisions of the Supreme Court on some of the key issues of this period.

Contraception and abortion

The campaign for the reform of contraception and abortion laws in America dates back to the early decades of the twentieth century. Until the 1960s reformers had concentrated their efforts on contraceptive rights, a far less emotive issue than that of abortion. Nevertheless, despite considerable success in persuading many state legislatures to make contraceptive devices freely available, the reform movement had made little headway in the federal courts. This was partly because the issue was deemed one which the Constitution left to the discretion of state governments and partly because there was no obvious clause in the Constitution which pertained to contraceptive rights. Thus respect for the traditional principles of federalism and the original meaning and text of the Constitution had persuaded the federal courts to exercise judicial self-restraint.

Griswold v. Connecticut (1965)

In 1965, however, the Supreme Court abandoned this restraint and made one of the most activist decisions in its history. Paradoxically, the case of *Griswold v. Connecticut* was highly contrived and, as far as contraceptive policy is concerned, quite insignificant. For Connecticut was the last State in the Union not to have liberalised its law on contraception. Its statute dated back to 1879 and criminalised the prescription and use of contraceptives. The law was hopelessly out of date by the 1960s and was not seriously enforced. Nevertheless, with a great deal of effort, members of the leading reformist group, Planned Parenthood, somehow managed to actually get themselves arrested and convicted for giving advice on contraception to a married couple.

When their conviction came to the Supreme Court on appeal, a 7–2 majority of the Justices declared the law unconstitutional. That was not too surprising, especially as even one of the dissenters, Justice Potter Stewart, described the Connecticut statute as 'uncommonly silly'. The great significance of the case, however, was that in striking down the law, the Court created a new constitutional right – that of privacy. Moreover, the new right was so vague that it was not at all clear exactly what else it might embrace. In short, the Court had created a new right that might allow the Justices to read into it almost anything they chose. In that sense, it was the perfect recipe for innovative judicial policy-making.

The Court's reasoning in *Griswold* was not entirely without historical support. As far back as the 1920s the Court had held that the Constitution protected certain rights not specifically mentioned in its text, that implicated the privacy or autonomy of individuals. Such 'unenumerated rights' included the right to educate one's children as one wished and, indeed, the right to have children in the first place.

In *Griswold*, however, Justice William O. Douglas's opinion for the Court went far beyond these sporadic cases and clearly set out to create a new constitutional weapon that could strike at numerous other laws that the Justices thought unreasonable. Although he acknowledged that the word 'privacy' was not even mentioned in the Constitution, Douglas argued that other clauses had 'penumbras and emanations' which altogether added up to a self-standing right of privacy. Never before (or since) had the Court created such a wholesale new right.

Although only two Justices dissented, their arguments persuaded many scholars. Justice Hugo Black, who was usually on the liberal side of constitutional disputes, derided the notion of a right to privacy, arguing that there was simply no constitutional basis for it: 'I like my privacy as well as the next one, but I am nevertheless compelled to admit that government has a right to invade it unless prohibited by some specific constitutional provision.'

As we shall see in Chapter Five, Justice Black was here invoking the traditional principle of judicial review that courts should only enforce rights which are explicitly mentioned or clearly implied in the text of the Constitution. Otherwise, Justices are in effect free to read their personal policy preferences into the Constitution. And indeed, that is precisely what Black thought the Court was doing in *Griswold*. He accused his colleagues in the majority of behaving precisely as had the reactionary conservatives of earlier decades who had employed substantive due process to read 'liberty of contract' and *laissez-faire* economics in the Fourteenth Amendment.

If Black had the better of the legal argument in *Griswold*, however, the decision caused little fuss. Like Brown, many believed that the Court had ushered in a much-needed reform. With the policy result so good, there was no widespread mood to take the Court to task for usurping the policy-making powers of the Connecticut legislature. In this respect, it seemed that the ends justified the means. And if elected politicians were failing to bring American law into line with contemporary enlightened opinion, then few objected when the Court led the way to reform.

The passivity with which the new judicial activism was greeted was only transformed, therefore, when the Court began to make policy choices that provoked widespread opposition. To be sure, the desegregation cases had been roundly condemned and resisted in the South: but such opposition was seen in the rest of the country as stemming from a bigoted and outdated vested interest to protect. In 1973, however, the Court set off a political storm over the issue of abortion rights which rages even today.

Roe v. Wade (1973)

A strong movement for the reform of America's nineteenth-century abortion laws began in the 1960s. As with contraception, abortion law was the responsibility of the States and most had chosen to ban abortion altogether, except where necessary to save the mother's life or safeguard her health. A variety of concerns, however, led to these laws being questioned. Doctors were disturbed by an increasing number of illegal, 'back-street' abortions performed by unqualified abortionists. Mental health specialists and social workers were concerned about the toll taken on women's and children's lives by numerous unwanted pregnancies. And both lawyers and doctors were anxious about the vagueness of abortion laws that rendered doctors vulnerable to prosecution for performing abortions which they thought were legal.

There was a growing feeling among professionals in the 1960s, then, that state abortion laws should be clarified and liberalised to give women and their doctors greater access to abortion on health grounds. This feeling was strengthened when women gave birth to a spate of severely deformed babies as a result of an outbreak of rubella (German Measles). Worse still were those babies born deformed as a result of their mothers having taken the prescribed drug thalidomide during pregnancy. One such mother, Sherri Finkbine, became famous in 1962 when she was refused an abortion in America for her thalidomide-damaged fetus and had to go abroad for her termination.

State politicians picked up on the mood for reform and about one-third of the States had liberalised their abortion laws by the early 1970s. Opposition to liberalised abortion was, at first, low-key. Controversy arose in the early 1970s, however, largely in response to the increasing impact on abortion policies of the movement for 'women's liberation'. The women's movement demanded a virtually unlimited right to abortion, claiming that reproductive autonomy was a precondition of sex equality. This changed the thrust of the abortion issue from one which was essentially concerned with health matters to one which was, in addition, highly politicised. In turn, this generated an opposition movement inspired not simply by a theological stand against abortion, but also by an anti-feminist conservatism.

A major political conflict was thus in the offing in 1973 when the Court decided to intervene in abortion policy in the case of Roe v. Wade. In so doing, the Court provoked the bitterest conflict in American politics of the past twenty-five years. The opinion for the Court majority of 7–2 was a blatant piece of judicial policy-making, in the sense that its constitutional (as opposed to political) basis was very weak. Based on the already dubious reasoning of the *Griswold* case, the Court flatly asserted that the right to privacy was broad enough to encompass a woman's right to choose an abortion.

Although the Court held that the embryo or fetus had no constitutional rights, it did maintain that the States had certain powers to protect potential life and also to preserve maternal health. The Court, therefore, produced a carefully calibrated set of regulations based, in part, on medical science. These said that during the first three months of pregnancy (the first trimester), the State could not intervene in the decision of a woman and her licensed doctor to opt for an abortion. In the second trimester, the State could regulate the conditions under which abortions took place, in order to preserve maternal health. In the third trimester, when the fetus was viable, that is, capable of living outside the womb, the State could actually ban abortions, except where this threatened the woman's life or health (see Table 1.3).

Table 1.3 The Supreme Court's abortion policy: balancing rights and interests in *Roe v. Wade* (1973)

	1st trimester	*2nd trimester*	*3rd trimester*
Woman's right	Free to choose abortion for any reason	Free to choose but subject to regulation	Free to choose on health grounds only
State's interests	No 'compelling interest'	Interest in protecting mother's health allows regulation, but not prohibition	Interest in protecting potential life justifies prohibition, except where woman's health/life endangered
Embryo/ Fetus	No rights or interests	No rights or interests	No rights or interests

Thus, since the vast majority of abortions are performed in the first and second trimesters of pregnancy, the practical meaning of *Roe* appeared to be that women now had a virtually unlimited right to choose an abortion. For many who sympathised with the cause of abortion reform, the *Roe* framework was excellent policy. For many judicial scholars, however, there was a major problem: there was almost no plausible constitutional basis for declaring a new right to abortion. Thus, as one actual supporter of abortion rights lamented, 'It is bad because it is bad constitutional law, or rather because it is *not* constitutional law and gives almost no sense of an obligation to try to be.'[3]

The Court's legal critics had plenty of ammunition. As well as the flimsy basis for the right to privacy itself, there was the problem of linking that right to abortion. After all, at least in the case of contraception, the only parties involved were consenting adults. Here, however, a potential human life was also involved. Thus privacy hardly seemed the appropriate concept on which to base abortion rights. The fact that the Court decided that a fetus was not a person within the meaning of the Constitution – and therefore had no rights – also made the ruling a morally dubious one for many.

There was also the problem of federalism. *Roe* effectively struck down virtually every abortion statute throughout the United States, reformed or otherwise. Thus *Roe* nationalised abortion policy, when until now policy had been determined by each State for itself.

Roe therefore marks the high point of the new judicial activism and the role of the Court as an agency of progressive social reform. But although *Roe* was in many ways in line with other judicial policy-making innovations of recent years, what made it different from the others was simply the issue it addressed. According to many people, *Roe* was simply bad policy and, more important still, these opponents felt more intensely about abortion than they did about contraception or other social issues. In other words, it was the substance of *Roe* that made it so controversial, but the sustained attack on the policy also generated an unusually determined attack upon the new policy-making role of the Court. Simply put, many thought the Court had gone too far and 'pro-life' interest groups were galvanised into active opposition to the *Roe* abortion policy. (See Chapter Six for developments in abortion policy since *Roe*.)

Capital punishment

One policy area in which the Court undoubtedly went too far for most of the nation was that of capital punishment. In the case of *Furman v. Georgia* (1972), a 5–4 majority of the Justices declared all existing death penalty statutes unconstitutional under the Eighth Amendment's ban on 'cruel and unusual punishments'.

There are several obvious reasons why this was a radical step by the Court. First, at the time of the *Furman* decision, thirty-nine States and the District of Columbia had the death penalty. It seemed difficult to argue, therefore, that the death penalty was considered either cruel or unusual in American culture.

Second, the Constitution made it very explicit that the framers considered capital punishment acceptable. For example, the Fifth and Fourteenth Amendments stated that no person should be deprived of life 'without due process of law': the obvious implication was that a person could be deprived of life provided due process standards were observed. The Fifth Amendment also states that 'No person shall be held to answer for a capital ... crime unless on a presentment or indictment of a Grand Jury.'

Third, the Supreme Court itself had recently ruled that the death penalty was permissible. Admittedly, it had held in *Trop v. Dulles* (1958) that the meaning of the Eighth Amendment's 'cruel and unusual punishments' clause was not permanently fixed, but rather drew its meaning from 'the evolving standards of decency that mark the progress of a maturing society'. In the same case, however, the Court explicitly denied that American society had evolved to the point where capital punishment could be considered unconstitutional.

Neither had the Justices changed their mind by the early 1970s. For in *McGautha v. California* (1971), the Court turned down even a partial attack on the constitutionality of California's death penalty statute when it ruled that the State was not obliged to provide separate trial and sentencing hearings in capital cases.

Finally, when the Court came to consider public opinion on the death penalty, it was clear that support for it was strong and rising. Although the widespread liberal mood of the early 1960s had seen an increase in those favouring the abolition of capital punishment, the pendulum had swung back in favour of retention by the time of the *Furman* decision. This was probably due to the rapid increase in the number of murders and other violent crimes in America in the latter part of the 1960s. Between 1967 and 1981, the number of murders rose by 61 per cent and other violent crimes by 80 per cent.[4] It came as no surprise, then, that in 1972 polls showed that those who favoured retention of the death penalty outnumbered those who supported abolition by 58 to 43 per cent.[5]

It seemed impossible therefore that, one year after *McGautha*, the Court in *Furman* could find sound constitutional reasons for striking down every death penalty statute in the country. Yet that is precisely what happened. Why did the Court take such a radical step?

The short answer is that five of the Justices of the Supreme Court simply decided that the nation needed a more enlightened punishment policy than that favoured by legislators, the public and the constitutional framers. For two of the Justices, Brennan and Marshall, the principal motivation was their belief that capital punishment was simply barbaric. Justice Brennan considered execution an affront to human dignity. Justice Marshall agreed and thought that polls showing a majority of the public in favour of retention reflected not the public's moral values but its ignorance of the facts about capital punishment:

> I cannot believe that at this stage in our history, the American people would ever knowingly support puposeless vengeance. Thus, I believe that the great mass of citizens would conclude on the basis of the material already considered that the death penalty is immoral and therefore unconstitutional.

From these standpoints, Brennan and Marshall concluded that the death penalty in all its forms was unconstitutional.

The other three Justices did not go quite as far, however. They declared all existing statutes unconstitutional because they allowed the death penalty to be imposed in an arbitrary and purposeless fashion. Justice Douglas made the point that it was the poor and the racial minorities who were most likely to be executed, while Justice Stewart thought the imposition of the penalty to be so random that 'These death sentences are cruel and unusual in the same way that being struck by lightning is cruel and unusual.' For his part, Justice White argued that the death penalty was so infrequently carried out that it did not serve any rational policy goal. As such, it amounted to 'the pointless and needless extinction of life with only marginal contributions to any discernible social or public purposes'.

Critically, however, Douglas, Stewart and White stopped short of saying that the death penalty was intrinsically and under all circumstances unconstitutional. Thus their opinions could be read as implying that the elimination of randomness in the imposition of the death penalty would render it constitutionally acceptable. Nevertheless, this was not the way *Furman* was understood outside the Court. Most commentators concluded that the death penalty had effectively been abolished in the United States and would never reappear.

For their part, the four dissenting Justices were not so much concerned about the apparent demise of capital punishment as they were about the use of judicial review to accomplish it. Justice Blackmun, for example, declared himself personally opposed to the death penalty, but argued that the Court had overstepped the mark separating constitutional interpretation from legislative policy-making. And Justice Powell deplored the damage the decision did to federalism, judicial restraint and the separation of powers, adding 'I can recall no case in which, in the name of deciding constitutional questions, this Court has subordinated national and democratic processes to such an extent.'

In taking it upon themselves to abolish the death penalty, the Supreme Court had gone out on a limb. Once again, it had introduced a major reform that was intended to make the United States a more just and enlightened society. Once again, however, the Court had instigated a policy which did not stem convincingly from constitutional interpretation or what many considered to be the appropriate role of an unelected judiciary in a democratic system. Once again, therefore, there was great tension between a 'good' result and the means by which it had been achieved. Moreover, the *Furman* result was more like *Roe* than *Brown* in that it generated passionate opposition throughout the country. (See Chapter Six for details of the reaction to *Furman*.) And in so doing, it focused even greater attention on the transformation of the role of the Supreme Court in American politics.

Reactions to the Court's new role

By the time of the Court's decisions in *Roe* and *Furman*, it had become clear that the federal judiciary was playing a political role quite different from its historical norm. It had, of course, been both activist and controversial before, but now it seemed to have embarked upon a sustained and wide-ranging agenda of reform. Sometimes this was with the support of public opinion and other branches of government, but sometimes not. And through it all, there was the constant theme that the Court's decisions were based less on genuine interpretation of the Constitution and more on liberal values drawn from elsewhere.

In effect, the Supreme Court had become a specialised agency for launching policy initiatives on certain kinds of civil rights and liberties issues. Moreover, the Court's dynamism engendered and accelerated its own momentum. Reformers soon spotted that the Court was open to new ideas and policies and began to see it as the best forum in which to pursue their goals. As well as those issues discussed above, the Court was urged to overturn laws affecting environmental policy, sex equality, affirmative action for racial minorites, gay rights, pornography, welfare and government support for religion.

The Court did not create the disputes over these issues, but it did try to resolve them through an expansive concept of judicial review; and to do so in ways that favoured the liberal or even radical side of the argument. Inevitably, therefore, the Court made enemies who were determined not only to oppose and reverse the Court's liberal policies, but also to force the Court to abandon its role as an agency of liberal reform.

We will see in the Chapter Six how these opponents often managed to undermine the Court's decisions by using other centres of power in the political system. But first, let us return to the Court's contemporary agenda to see how the conservative backlash made itself felt in the Justices' decisions.

Affirmative action

The *Brown* decision dealt with the issue of legal, or *de jure*, race discrimination and, eventually, this was brought to an end. But what *Brown* and similar cases did not accomplish was an end to racial inequality, or even to racial segregation in some respects. Centuries of legal racial discrimination created enormous economic and social disadvantages which live on long after the laws themselves have been abolished. This so-called *de facto* discrimination (resulting from socio-economic realities rather than intentionally discriminatory laws), condemned most blacks to be second-class citizens. Amongst other things, African-Americans suffer from much poorer housing conditions (in often racially separate neighbourhoods), and inferior educational opportunities (in predominantly black schools), health care and employment prospects than white Americans (see Table 1.4). Moreover, there is still evidence of private discrimination against black Americans, unconscious or otherwise.

In the 1960s, therefore, the United States government decided that something called 'affirmative action' was necessary to improve the social and economic equality of African-Americans. At first, this took the form of making a special effort to recruit blacks into jobs or universities that had previously been closed to them. Gradually, however, businesses, government agencies and universities began to reserve a specific number of positions for African-Americans and other racial minorities.

These policies were successful in giving racial minorities better educational and employment opportunities. But whites soon began to complain about 'reverse discrimination'. They pointed out, for example, that some successful minority college applicants had lower grades than white applicants who had been rejected. They claimed, therefore, that affirmative action programmes discriminated against them on the grounds of their race. In one of the great ironies of modern American constitutional law, they alleged that this violated the rights of whites under the Equal Protection clause of the Fourteenth Amendment – the clause which had originally been adopted to protect blacks from discrimination by whites!

Table 1.4 Indices of racial inequality

1. Poverty: percentages living below the poverty line, 1990

Region	White (%)	Black (%)	Black multiple
Northeast	9.9	31.6	3.19
Midwest	10.1	35.7	3.53
South	12.4	34.1	2.75
West	13.5	24.4	1.81

2. Health: causes of death, black rates as multiples of white rates, 1990

Homicide	6.76
Tuberculosis	6.66
Pregnancy	4.00
Anaemia	3.57
Meningitis	3.50
HIV-AIDS	3.22
Diabetes	2.42
Infant death	2.41
Drug-induced	1.83
Car accident	0.98
Suicide	0.57

3. Education: percentages of black pupils in predominantly white schools (selected cities 1986–87)

Colorado Springs, Col.	88.6
San Jose, Cal.	67.6
Albuquerque, N.M.	51.8
Toledo, Oh.	34.2
Seattle, Wash.	25.8
Philadelphia, Pa.	10.6
New York, N.Y.	6.8
Los Angeles, Cal.	4.9
Dallas, Tex.	4.6
Chicago, Ill.	2.4

Source: Data adapted from A. Hacker, *Two Nations: Black and White, Separate, Hostile, Unequal* (expanded edn), New York, 1995, pp. 251–62.

The battle over the rights and wrongs of affirmative action has raged at both state and federal level in the United States. And because, one way or another, affirmative action implicated the rights protected by the Equal Protection clause, the Supreme Court found it impossible to avoid the issue.

Race and higher education

The first major case came in 1978, in *Regents of the University of California v. Bakke*. Here a white student, Allan Bakke, had failed to gain a place at the Davis Medical School. Davis had an affirmative action programme which reserved sixteen places for disadvantaged students, all of whom in practice turned out to be members of ethnic minority groups. Bakke, whose grades were higher than all the applicants admitted under the affirmative action programme, claimed he had been denied a place at the Medical School solely because of his race and hence had been deprived of his rights under the Equal Protection clause of the Fourteenth Amendment.

The issue of affirmative action is one fraught with difficulty, as most people would concede that there are merits on both sides of the argument. On the one hand, African-Americans had suffered centuries of the most appalling discrimination and some kind of remedial action seems wholly in order. Given this history of disadvantage, it hardly seems inappropriate to give blacks a modest level of advantage as a means of achieving a greater measure of racial equality. Moreover, as a practical matter, affirmative action is a relatively quick and effective means of getting more African-Americans into good jobs and universities.

On the other hand, Allan Bakke himself had never been responsible for racial discrimination. Yet he was now being denied a place at Davis because of the discrimination of others. In addition, the theory of the Equal Protection clause and, indeed, American ideology, is that race should be irrelevant to a person's status and opportunities. The United States holds itself to be a meritocratic society, where individuals may not be held back by race. If the goal is thus to create a 'colour-blind' society, it makes no sense to replace racial disadvantages for blacks with racial disadvantages for whites or any other group.

In the *de jure* segregation and discrimination cases of the 1950s and 1960s, the constitutional arguments were relatively straightforward. Even if the framers of the Equal Protection clause had not intended to abolish segregated schools, the Court could argue quite powerfully that the principle of equality in the modern era required government to treat people of all races in the same way.

This interpretation of equality sits rather uneasily, however, with government programmes designed to give advantages to racial minorities, even if their aim is to achieve racial equality in the long term. In short, the constitutional reasoning in *Brown v. Board of Education* did not give very clear guidance in cases involving affirmative action. Government was following *Brown* in the sense that it was trying to promote racial equality, but departing from *Brown* in treating whites and blacks differently.

The nine Justices of the Supreme Court were now being asked to reconcile these two positions – seemingly an impossible task. Unsurprisingly, and as often happens in such difficult cases, the Justices could not agree and produced a decision which settled very little about the constitutionality of affirmative action.

Four Justices were clear that the Davis programme did not violate the Fourteenth Amendment and that preferential treatment for African-Americans was not to be viewed with the same suspicion as policies that sought to stigmatise blacks or any other racial group. Affirmative action designed to remedy past discrimination was thus acceptable, because its ultimate goal was equality of the races, not inequality.

Four of the other Justices were equally clear that the Davis programme was *not* acceptable and that Bakke was entitled to a place in the Medical School. Their argument was based mainly on the fact that American law was straightforward: no person could suffer disdadvantage because of race, whatever the ultimate goal of that disadvantage was. The colour-blind principle must be applied.

This left Justice Lewis Powell with the deciding vote. He agreed that the Fourteenth Amendment banned numerical quotas of the kind employed by the Davis Medical School. He also reasoned, therefore, that Allan Bakke was entitled to a place at Davis.

Powell then decided, however, that the principle of remedial affirmative action was sound, provided that race was not the sole factor in any preference programme. In other words, a minority applicant's race could be counted as a positive factor among many others in gaining a place at a university. However, no places could be reserved exclusively for members of any particular ethnic group. In short, racial quotas were out, but remedial race preference was in.

That said, however, *Bakke* left a great deal about affirmative action open to question. In the first place, the vote was so tight that the retirement or death of just one Justice might produce an entirely different result in the next case. Protagonists on both sides could continue to hope for a clear-cut victory, therefore.

Moreover, the lack of clarity in the decision as to how much weight could be given to race was a problem. For example, could so much weight be attached to race that quotas could still effectively, though unofficially, operate? Or could so little weight be attached to race that some universities might not take any effective measures to promote greater racial equality?

It is quite possible that Justice Powell was hoping that his Opinion would be acclaimed as an act of statesmanship and that his refusal to hand total victory to either side of the political conflict would make a satisfactory compromise. But as the abortion and death penalty cases amply demonstrate, where a substantial and bitter political conflict exists, the Supreme Court cannot impose a resolution on the warring factions.

Affirmative action in the workplace

So the political and judicial battle over affirmative action continued. In the 1980s, the Court was asked to decide cases which were even more politically sensitive than *Bakke*. For by now, many government agencies and private companies were operating affirmative action programmes that affected their policies on the hiring, firing and promotion of employees. And while it may be upsetting not to obtain a place in the university of one's choice, it is far more serious to lose one's job because of a race-preference policy.

The Court muddled through these cases as best it could. In *Wygant v. Board of Education* (1986), for example, a 5–4 majority of the Justices decided that an affirmative action plan which led to lay-offs of white teachers who had more seniority than minority teachers who were retained, was unconstitutional. The Court decided that the loss of their jobs imposed too great a burden of remedial action on the white teachers.

In 1989, opponents of affirmative action won another victory in *Richmond v. Croson*. This involved the type of affirmative action plan known as 'set-asides'. This particular plan required that 30 per cent of the value of city construction contracts must be set aside for minority-owned businesses. The aim was to give minority businesses a share of contracts that had always gone almost exclusively to white-owned businesses.

Nevertheless, in spite of its ostensibly remedial purpose, the Court declared the Richmond plan unconstitutional by a vote of 6 to 3. The majority Justices were concerned that Richmond had no documented evidence of past racial discrimination in the local construction industry. Moreover, they thought the 30 per cent set aside was arbitrary because far fewer than 30 per cent of local construction companies were owned by minorities. They saw no justification, therefore, for depriving white-owned businesses of the opportunity of bidding for the set-aside contracts.

Throughout the history of its affirmative action cases, the Court had always been willing to allow the Congress greater scope for affirmative action than it permitted state or local government bodies. This is because the Fourteenth Amendment puts a special responsibility on Congress for its enforcement. In 1995, however, in *Adarand v. Pena*, the Court dealt another blow to affirmative action by ruling 5 to 4 that Congress had no more leeway than any other legislative body. The Court did not actually decide whether the federal set-asides involved in *Adarand* were unconstitutional. Nor did it say that set-asides could never be justified by a proven history of discrimination in the relevant industries. But by subjecting Congress to the same strict judicial scrutiny applied to the city of Richmond in *Croson*, it makes it less likely that federal affirmative action plans will be upheld by the Court.

We can see, then, that the attempted compromise on affirmative action that was advanced in *Bakke* has largely failed. True, the most extreme opponents of affirmative action have not had their way and seen all race preferences declared unconstitutional. But there is equally no doubt that the Supreme Court is much tougher on affirmative action today than it was in the late 1970s. What has brought about this change?

Once again, the answer to this lies in the realm of politics. First, the country as a whole has swung to the right since *Bakke* was decided in 1978. More specifically, the country has become more antagonistic to affirmative action: a *Newsweek* poll of March 1995 revealed that 79 per cent of whites were opposed to race preferences and even minority members only supported them 50–46 per cent.

This shift in public mood has led many politicians to attack affirmative action and they have been rewarded by election to public office.

Moreover, there have been other avenues of attack, such as the California Civil Rights Initiative, passed by the State's voters in a referendum in November, 1996. This seeks to prohibit any and all programmes involving race preferences in the State. Although such political hostility to affirmative action may not directly influence the Court's deliberations, it does create an environment in which it is more difficult to take contentious decisions.

The California Civil Rights Initiative
State Referendum, November 1996

(a) The state shall not discriminate against, or grant preferential treatment to, any individual or group on the basis of race, sex, colour, ethnicity, or national origin in the operation of public employment, public education, or public contracting.

...

(c) Nothing in this section shall be interpreted as prohibiting bona fide qualifications based on sex which are reasonably necessary to the normal operation of public employment, public education, or public contracting.

...

(e) Nothing in this section shall be taken as prohibiting action which must be taken to establish or maintain eligibility for any federal programme, where ineligibility would result in the loss of federal funds to the state.

(f) For the purposes of this section, 'state' shall include, but not necessarily be limited to, the state itself, any city, county, city and county, public university system, including the University of California, community college district, school district, special district, or any other political subdivision or governmental instrumentality of or within the state.

(g) The remedies available for violations of this section shall be the same, regardless of the injured party's race, sex, colour, ethnicity, or national origin, as are otherwise available for violations of then-existing California anti-discrimination law.

(h) This section shall be self-executing. If any part or parts of this section are found to be in conflict with federal law or the United States Constitution, the section shall be implemented to the maximum extent that federal law and the United States Constitution permit. Any provision held invalid shall be severable from the remaining portions of this section.

More concrete, however, is the fact that a series of conservative electoral victories have enabled presidents to appoint new members to the

Court who are, to say the least, sceptical about the constitutionality of affirmative action. Thus the two Justices most opposed to affirmative action are Antonin Scalia, appointed by President Reagan in 1986, and Clarence Thomas, appointed by President Bush in 1991. Also usually found in the voting bloc against the constitutionality of affirmative action are Sandra Day O'Connor (Reagan, 1981), Anthony Kennedy (Reagan, 1987) and William Rehnquist (Nixon, 1972; elevated to Chief Justice by Reagan, 1986).

Voting blocs on the Supreme Court, 1994 Term: % of cases in which each Justice votes with others

Judge	R	St	O'C	Sc	Ke	So	Th	Gi	Br
Rehnquist	–	51	77	80	84	69	81	67	67
Stevens	51	–	55	45	61	69	42	75	71
O'Connor	77	55	–	68	76	77	67	65	74
Scalia	80	45	68	–	75	60	88	60	59
Kennedy	84	61	76	75	–	73	73	77	72
Souter	69	69	77	60	73	–	59	80	83
Thomas	81	42	67	88	73	56	–	54	59
Ginsburg	67	75	65	60	77	80	54	–	83
Breyer	67	71	74	59	72	83	59	83	–

These figures indicate the existence of voting alliances and blocs on the Court. Thus the pair of Justices most likely to agree with each other are Justices Scalia and Thomas, who voted together in 88 per cent of the cases during the 1994 Term. The least likely to agree are Justices Stevens and Thomas, who voted together in only 42 per cent of cases. If we place these two at opposite ends of the spectrum, we get an approximate left-right pattern as follows:

Left	**Centre**	**Right**
Stevens		Thomas
Ginsburg		Scalia
Breyer		Rehnquist
Souter	Kennedy	
	O'Connor	

Source: Adapted from Harvard Law Review, CIX, no. 1, 1995, p. 341.

Majority-minority districts

In the 1995 Term, the five Justices mentioned above came together to undermine yet another facet of affirmative action policy, the 'majority-minority' legislative district. In an attempt to increase the number of ethnic minority members of Congress, many States have drawn electoral boundaries which contain a majority of African-American or Hispanic voters. Using computers and street-by-street information on the race of residents, States conjured up some very strangely shaped congressional districts. Nevertheless, after the 1990 national population census and the associated re-districting exercise, the creation of many more majority-minority districts led to a significant increase in the number of minority members of Congress. The 1992 congressional elections saw the number of African-American members rise from twenty-six to thirty-nine and the number of Hispanic members from thirteen to eighteen.[6]

In a series of 5–4 decisions, however, the Supreme Court has ruled that it is unconstitutional under the Equal Protection clause of the Fourteenth Amendment to use race as the predominant criterion in re-districting, at least if other traditional criteria are subordinated to it. The Court first announced its intention to examine rigorously these majority-minority districts in *Shaw v. Reno* (1993). Speaking for the Court, Justice O'Connor argued that these districts were reminiscent of the worst racial gerrymanders of America's inglorious history of white supremacy and even likened them to apartheid.

When the Court came to decide on the actual substance of majority-minority districts, none of those under challenge survived. In *Miller v. Johnson* (1995), *Bush v. Vera* (1996) and *Shaw v. Hunt* (1996), the Court struck down majority-minority districts in Georgia, Texas and North Carolina respectively. The Court has not held that all majority-minority districts will necessarily be deemed unconstitutional. But it has made clear in yet another area of policy, that even well-intentioned racial classifications, designed to improve the political and economic position of minorities, will struggle to survive strict judicial scrutiny.

The affirmative action cases of recent years thus provide further support for the view that not only do great political issues become transformed into judicial cases, but also that political developments, including presidential elections and subsequent new appointments to the Court, influence the long-term outcome of those cases.

Government and religion

The issue of religious freedom has always been of great importance to Americans. Indeed, the desire to escape religious persecution in Europe was the main motivation to emigrate for many early settlers in the American colonies. Unsurprisingly, therefore, the framers of the Constitution incorporated guarantees of religious freedom into the Bill of Rights. The pertinent part of the First Amendment reads: 'Congress shall make no law respecting an establishment of religion, or prohibiting the free exercise thereof ...'.

Originally, the First Amendment applied only to Congress, leaving the states free to determine their own religious policies. As a result, during the first 150 years of the Constitution of 1789, the Supreme Court decided few cases under the religious clauses of the First Amendment. In the 1940s, however, this changed as the Court decided that both the 'Free Exercise clause' and the 'Establishment clause' were applicable to the States.[7] These cases were part of a broader trend of incorporating most of the Bill of Rights into the Fourteenth Amendment and thus making the Bill of Rights applicable to the States.

Incorporation of the Bill of Rights (1791) into the Fourteenth Amendment (1868)

In *Barron v. Baltimore* (1833), the Supreme Court held that the Bill of Rights was not applicable to the States. Thus, while the federal government could not abridge, say, freedom of speech, the state governments were free to do so if they wished. Some in the South, for example, banned publications which were critical of slavery.

In the twentieth century, however, the Supreme Court gradually 'incorporated' most of the Bill of Rights into the Fourteenth Amendment's Due Process clause. In effect, the Court argued that the Due Process clause required the States to observe federal standards whenever the deprivation of life, liberty or property was concerned. For this reason, we often speak of 'the nationalisation of the Bill of Rights'.

Some parts of the Bill of Rights have not yet been incorporated, but nearly all of its most important rights were nationalised either in the 1940s or the 1960s. Apart from expanding the civil liberties of citizens, the establishment of federal standards for the States is also very significant because it entailed an expansion of the power of the Supreme Court and the federal government in general. Here is a list of some of the key incorporation decisions.

Clause	Decision to incorporate
First Amendment	
free speech	*Gitlow v. New York* (1925)
freedom of assembly	*DeJonge v. Oregon* (1937)
free exercise of religion	*Cantwell v. Connecticut* (1940)
Establishment clause	*Everson v. Board of Education* (1947)
Fourth Amendment	
unreasonable search and seizure	*Wolf v. Colorado* (1949)
exclusionary rule	*Mapp v. Ohio* (1961)
Fifth Amendment	
self-incrimination	*Malloy v. Hogan* (1964)
double jeopardy	*Benton v. Maryland* (1969)
Sixth Amendment	
public trial	*In re Oliver* (1948)
right to counsel	*Gideon v. Wainwright* (1963)
jury trial	*Duncan v. Louisiana* (1968)
Eighth Amendment	
cruel and unusual punishment	*Louisiana ex rel. Francis* v. *Resweber* (1947)

These decisions also coincided with an increasing secularisation of American life that, amongst other things, encouraged the idea that religious belief was a private matter and that it should play little or no part in public life. This secular trend, however, had to encounter the fact that American public life was riddled with religious symbols, values and practices. All American money bears the statement 'In God we trust', sessions of Congress begin with a prayer and surely the most common utterance by American politicians, particularly on the campaign trail, is 'God bless America'. More significantly, government gave financial support to religious institutions, especially parochial schools, and religious values were imbued into Americans through public education and social policy.

These many and complex relationships between government and religion explain why the Establishment clause has given rise to many more controversial constitutional issues than the Free Exercise clause. On the whole, government in America is happy to see religions flourish and rarely tries to inhibit religious freedom. Civil liberties groups are equally comfortable with freedom of religious thought and practice.

It is thus only when religion encounters and becomes entangled with government institutions and policies that the clash between secular and religious values becomes constitutionally problematic. For this raises the question of whether government support or endorsement of religion constitutes an 'establishment of religion' prohibited by the First Amendment.

As with most constitutional terms, there is no clear or agreed definition of an 'establishment of religion'. No one disputes that it prohibits the creation of an official state religion, such as the Church of England, or the Catholic Church in the Irish Republic. Nor indeed is there much disagreement with the proposal that government in America must not give preference to one religion over another. On the other hand, while some such as current Chief Justice Rehnquist and Justice Scalia would stop about there and permit routine government 'accommodation' of religion, others subscribe to Thomas Jefferson's famous statement that the Establishment clause erected 'a wall of separation' between church and state. Such a wall would end virtually all contact between religion and government.

To complicate matters still further for the Court, there is considerable support amongst the American people not merely for religion and religious practice, but for the infusion of all aspects of life, public and private, with religious values. Elected politicians, either through personal conviction or electoral necessity, tend also to support religious values in the face of secular challenge. The net result is that the Court has sought to interpret and apply a constitutional clause which, while uncertain in meaning, touches upon a very sensitive nerve in American culture and public life.

The most enduring controversy initiated by the modern Court's Establishment clause jurisprudence was that involving school prayer. In *Engel v. Vitale* (1962) the Supreme Court struck down a non-denominational prayer which began the day in New York State's public school system. Although no pupil was compelled to recite the prayer, the Court ruled 7 to 1 that the State was attempting to encourage religion in a way that was inconsistent with the prohibition on the establishment of religion.

The following year, the Court exacerbated the public furore that greeted *Engel* by ruling in *Abington School District v. Schempp* (1963) that a Pennsylvania law requiring ten verses of the Bible to be read at the start of the school day was unconstitutional. Eight Justices agreed that such sponsorship of religion by the State was proscribed by the Establishment clause.

The Court's school prayer decisions were, and still are, deeply unpopular with the public, many politicians and most religious organisations. Indeed, in a country where 95 per cent of the population believe in God and some 60 per cent belong to a religious organisation, it comes as no surprise to learn that in a 1991 opinion poll, 78 per cent of Americans support the reintroduction of school prayer.[8] Such strong popular opposition to the Court's decisions almost inevitably led to literally hundreds of attempts to overturn them by constitutional amendment, as well as by the passage of state legislation seeking to circumvent them. Yet the ban on school prayer continues to this day.

The Court has been able to withstand the onslaught in part because it has allies amongst some important interest groups, especially the American Civil Liberties Union (ACLU) and some leading Jewish organisations. The Court can also rely upon the support and votes of a solid minority of liberal members of Congress who sympathise with the substance of the Justices' decisions.

The most important reason for the survival of the school prayer decisions, however, is that many members of Congress are reluctant to weaken the Court by such a wholesale attack on judicial supremacy in constitutional interpretation. Although they take electoral risks in refusing to support constitutional amendments that have overwhelming public backing, they are also aware that seriously to weaken the Court's authority on one issue may impair its willingness to defend other important, but unpopular, civil liberties. The Court thus benefits from the belief of many legislators that the country needs a strong champion of constitutional rights, in order that all who may one day find themselves in an unpopular minority may rely upon the Justices to defend their liberty.

The Supreme Court has therefore been able to expand upon its school prayer rulings. For example, in *Wallace v. Jaffree* (1985) a 6–3 majority of the Justices ruled unconstitutional an Alabama statute

mandating a period of silence at the start of the school day for the purposes of 'meditation or voluntary prayer'. And in *Lee v. Weisman*
(1992), the Court struck down the practice of having a religious bene-
diction read out at a high-school graduation ceremony.

It should be emphasised that the Court has not been invariably hostile to state involvement with religion. In 1969, in *Board of Education
v. Allen*, the Justices upheld a law requiring public school districts to
lend secular books to religious schools. And in *Zobrest v. Catalina
Foothills District* (1993), the Court ordered the state of Arizona to
extend its provision of sign-language interpreters to deaf schoolchildren in public schools to religious schools.

Nevertheless, if the Supreme Court has not made Jefferson's 'wall
of separation' into an insuperable obstacle preventing all state accommodation of religious expression, it has ensured that no direct governmental support of religion is permitted. This is true even in
relatively trivial matters. For example, in *Lynch v. Donnelly* (1984), the
city of Pawtucket, R.I., erected its traditional Christmas display which
featured religious figures, such as the infant Jesus, Mary and Joseph
and angels, as well as secular symbols of the season, including Santa
Claus and a Christmas tree. Five Justices of the Supreme Court
thought the display had the primarily secular purpose of celebrating
Christmas as a holiday for all Americans, regardless of religious belief.

Five years later, however, in *Allegheny County v. Pittsburgh ACLU*,
Justice O'Connor voted with the four *Lynch* dissenters to strike down
Allegheny County's Christmas display because it contained only religious figures and a banner proclaiming 'Gloria in Excelsis Deo'. Justice Blackmun explained the difference as follows: '*Lynch* teaches that
government may celebrate Christmas in some manner and form, but
not in a way that endorses Christian doctrine. Here Allegheny County
has transgressed that line. It has chosen to celebrate Christmas in a
way that has the effect of endorsing a patently Christian message:
Glory to God for the birth of Jesus Christ.'

These two cases reveal some important facts about the Supreme
Court. First, they highlight the difference one Justice can make when
the rest of the Court is evenly divided. Here, Justice O'Connor provided the swing vote. Second, they demonstrate the significance of the
factual circumstances of a case when the Court is applying a broad
constitutional principle. This is particularly important for interest
groups who seek a Court decision on a broad principle, for the outcome may well depend on whether they have selected a case with

favourable or unfavourable facts. It is for this reason that groups often search very carefully and for a long time before selecting the right case through which to bring an issue before the Court.

If the Christmas display cases may be considered somewhat trivial in substance, the broad principle they involved is not. The cases are worthy of attention, therefore, because they help to develop the meaning of a constitutional principle which will be applied in other cases of far greater substantive significance. For example, in the 1970s and 1980s, groups associated with the New Christian Right had launched a campaign to force public schools to teach 'Creation Science'. The principal feature of Creation Science is the belief in the Bible's account of the origins of the earth and its species that is contained in the Book of Genesis. Creation scientists hold not merely that God created the world in six days, but that this can be proven scientifically. As such, it stands opposed to the Darwinian orthodoxy that the planet and life developed according to certain principles of evolution. Here, then, is the ultimate conflict between religion and secularism in education.

Some States had actually sought to ban the teaching of Darwinism altogether, but the Supreme Court had declared that unconstitutional in *Epperson v. Arkansas* (1968). Now, however, the resurgent Christian fundamentalist movement sought to require Creation Science to be taught alongside Darwinism as a theory of equal value. In 1981 Louisiana passed the Balanced Treatment Act, which enshrined this approach in law.

With only Chief Justice Rehnquist and Justice Scalia dissenting, however, the Court declared the law unconstitutional in *Edwards v. Aguillard* (1987). Speaking for the Court, Justice Brennan described the Act's alleged goal of advancing academic freedom as a sham, and insisted that it was nothing less than an attempt to advance a religious belief. Therefore, he wrote, 'The Act violates the Establishment clause of the First Amendment because it seeks to employ the symbolic and financial support of government to achieve a religious purpose.'

The Establishment clause of the First Amendment has spawned hundreds of cases and the Supreme Court has sometimes struggled to maintain a clear and consistent set of principles to resolve them. In that sense, they serve to remind us that judicial review often requires the Justices to possess the art of muddling through the constitutional and political complexities that present themselves. It is also imperative, however, not to lose sight of the main picture. For the Establishment clause cases involve nothing less than the attempt by nine

Justices to preserve, and adapt to the modern era, the spirit of one of the great founding principles of American government: that in order to ensure freedom from religious persecution, government must not throw its weight behind religious belief. And for all the inevitable disagreement and controversy that this task arouses, it is the foremost justification for the principle of judicial review and the power of the Supreme Court.

Gay and lesbian rights

No issue demonstrates the dynamic nature of the Supreme Court's agenda better than that of the rights of homosexuals. When Justice Stone penned his famous Footnote Four over fifty years ago, not even he would have dreamt that the 'discrete and insular minorites' to be given special judicial protection should include homosexuals.

Today, however, the status and rights of gays and lesbians in the United States is a major political and, therefore of course, legal controversy. A combination of factors has brought these issues to the fore. In the first place, the general increase in tolerance towards non-conformity that began in the 1960s has included a more sympathetic understanding of homosexuality. This does not mean that homosexuality is generally accepted, but rather that it is increasingly tolerated. As a result, there is a significant percentage of Americans who now believe that laws which discriminate against gays and lesbians are wrong. Thus, a 1990 review of opinion polls revealed that while three-quarters of Americans believed that sexual acts between gays and lesbians were morally wrong, a majority, 47–36 per cent, thought that such acts should not be illegal. Moreover, a 1996 *Newsweek* poll showed that 33 per cent of respondents believed that same-sex marriages should be recognised in law, although 58 per cent remained opposed.

The most important factor in the rise of homosexuality as a political factor is, however, the actions of gays and lesbians themselves. A 'gay pride' movement emerged in the late 1960s, determined to convince homosexuals and, indeed, all Americans, that homosexuality was a legitimate, morally acceptable lifestyle and that laws which discriminate on the basis of sexual orientation violated the Constitution.

The gay rights movement followed the example of the civil rights movement and sought favourable decisions from the federal courts. On the surface, at least, they stood a good chance of success. Gays and lesbians had long been despised and discriminated against by American law and culture, and hence were in need of protection from majority prejudice. They also could expect to benefit from the Court's creation of a new constitutional right to privacy in 1965. Although the right to privacy had never been applied to gay rights, its spirit was the belief that individuals had the right to decide for themselves the intimate details of their lives. This notion of personal autonomy – a freedom from governmental interference in one's private life – seemed highly applicable to a number of issues related to sexual orientation.

On the other hand, in the 1980s many state laws still criminalised gay and lesbian sexual acts and there was little or no protection for homosexuals who suffered discrimination in employment, housing, health insurance and a host of other matters.

Here then was a classic combination of factors that urged the Supreme Court into action: social and cultural currents which signalled changing values; a political movement dedicated to transforming longstanding laws, but which was countered by deeply-held values and prejudices; a prominent political and cultural struggle between these contending forces; and a constitutional doctrine that was unclear, but which offered some hope to the insurgent faction.

Nevertheless, precisely because the issue of gay rights was so politically controversial, the Supreme Court was not anxious to become embroiled in it. Moreover, as we have seen, the Court in the 1980s was undergoing a change in personnel: the more liberal judges of recent decades were being replaced by Republican appointees of a conservative legal and political persuasion. There was little hope, therefore, of the Court producing a decisive resolution of the issues.

Thus it proved in 1986 when the Court decided *Bowers v. Hardwick*. Michael Hardwick had been prosecuted and convicted for engaging in homosexual acts in his own home in Atlanta, Georgia. He appealed on the grounds that Georgia's anti-sodomy statute was an unconstitutional invasion of his right to privacy. He won his appeal in the lower federal court, whereupon the State's Attorney General Michael Bowers brought an appeal in defence of the statute to the Supreme Court.

Predictably the vote of the Justices was close, but a 5–4 majority decided against Hardwick. Although the minority Justices argued that the right to privacy should logically include harmless private acts conducted in one's private home, the majority believed that the State had the right to ban sexual acts which it considered socially damaging.

They further argued that, despite the decriminalisation of sodomy in many States in recent years, there was still no consensus to support the conclusion that the liberty to engage in homosexual acts was a 'fundamental right' protected by the Constitution.

The *Bowers* case was clearly a setback for the gay rights movement, even though Justice Lewis Powell, who had voted with the majority, acknowledged after his retirement from the Court that he should have voted the other way. Nevertheless, the issues involved in gay rights were too politically insistent to disappear. Thus, a row erupted in 1993 when President Clinton proposed ending the ban on gays and lesbians serving in the armed forces. Such was the hostility of the reaction from the military and many members of Congress that Clinton backed off. Eventually, a compromise was reached whereby the military would no longer ask service personnel whether they were homosexual and also would not take active measures to discover their sexual orientation. Gay personnel, however, were required not to openly announce their sexual orientation. This is the so-called 'Don't Ask, Don't Tell' policy currently in force.

While there may be political merits to such a compromise, the policy creates constitutional problems that the Supreme Court will eventually have to resolve. Indeed, several cases (at the time of writing) are currently in the lower courts because the policy appears to restrict the free speech rights of homosexual service personnel, rights protected by the First Amendment. On the other hand, the Supreme Court has always shown considerable deference to armed forces chiefs, who need considerable discretion in deciding how best to run the nation's vital defence forces. Once again, then, a political and cultural conflict has been transformed into a judicial problem because of the need to resolve competing constitutional claims. As things stand, it is anyone's guess how the Court will decide this thorny question.

The political and legal impetus behind the debate over gay rights continues in other respects as well. For example, the Supreme Court of Hawaii ruled in *Baehr v. Lewin* (1993) that the State's refusal to issue marriage licences to same-sex couples will be deemed to violate the State Constitution's Equal Protection Clause, unless the state government can demonstrate a 'compelling' reason for doing so. But whatever the final decision in that case in the Hawaiin courts, it is almost bound to come on appeal to the US Supreme Court.

The Court's task, however, will be further complicated by the passage in 1996 of The Defence of Marriage Act. This bans federal recognition of gay marriages and absolves States from their usual obligation to honour other States' legal proceedings. This obligation stems from the 'Full Faith and Credit clause' of Article IV of the Constitution. The Supreme Court may thus find itself caught in a constitutional conflict between the Equal Protection clause and the Full Faith and Credit clause; and in a political conflict between the gay rights movement and moral traditionalists over same-sex marriage.

The Defence of Marriage Act 1996

Section 2 (a) ... No State, territory, or possession of the United States, or Indian Tribe, shall be required to give effect to any public act, record, or judicial proceeding of any other State, territory, possession, or tribe respecting a relationship between persons of the same sex that is treated as a marriage under the laws of such other State, territory, possession, or tribe, or a right or claim arising from such relationship.

...

Section 3 (a) ... In determining the meaning of any Act of Congress, or of any ruling, regulation, or interpretation of the various administrative bureaus and agencies of the United States, the word 'marriage' means only a legal union between one man and one woman as husband and wife, and the word 'spouse' refers only to a person of the opposite sex who is a husband or wife.

One issue that has already made its way to the Court is that of state anti-discrimination legislation which protect gays and lesbians. In 1996, in *Romer v. Evans*, the Supreme Court entered the thick of the battle over gay rights that has been raging in Colorado for a number of years. The gay rights movement had been successful in cities such as Denver, Aspen and Boulder in persuading local legislative councils to pass ordinances forbidding discrimination on grounds of sexual orientation. Forces opposed to these measures took their cause to the level of the State by campaigning for an amendment to the State constitution which would prohibit all laws and policies which gave such protection to gays and lesbians. Amendment 2, as it was known, was passed by a popular referendum in 1992, by a vote of 54–46 per cent.

The response of the gay rights movement was to move up to the federal level of power and ask the Supreme Court to rule that Amendment 2 violated the Equal Protection clause of the Fourteenth Amendment to the US Constitution. Thus a political struggle that had begun in municipalities in Colorado ended up on the agenda of the Supreme Court in Washington.

The only major precedent on gay rights was *Bowers*, a case in which, as we saw, the Court refused to acknowledge that there was any constitutional legitimacy to homosexual acts. Nevertheless, in *Romer v. Evans*, a 6–3 majority of the Court literally ignored the *Bowers* case and declared Amendment 2 unconstitutional. Justice Kennedy's Opinion for the Court argued that the Amendment, in singling out homosexuals and no other group as the object of a ban on protective legislation, had been motivated by nothing other than animosity towards gays and lesbians. And without any further justification for the ban, the Amendment violated the constitutional requirement for the equal treatment of all persons.

The majority did not go so far as to say that discrimination against gays and lesbians was on a par with discrimination against racial minorities or women. In the latter cases, the Supreme Court requires government to offer very strong justifications for treating people differently from others, but in *Romer* the Court studiously avoided saying the same of homosexuals.

This, combined with the awkward silence on the *Bowers* case, left the Court's reasoning vulnerable to attack by the dissenting Justices. In fact, Justice Antonin Scalia said squarely that if *Bowers* allowed homosexual conduct to be criminalised, then it surely cannot be unconstitutional for Colorado merely to disfavour homosexuals in other policy areas. He also pointed out that the Court had always held that laws banning polygamy were constitutional, thus demonstrating that States could ban or disfavour sexual conduct they deemed morally harmful.

What Scalia's dissenting Opinion revealed, then, was that there was no escape from the underlying question presented in *Romer*: is homosexuality a morally or socially harmful practice or is it simply an alternative sexual orientation that threatens no one? If the former, then States may disfavour it; but if the latter, any discrimination against gays and lesbians is irrational prejudice and quite unacceptable under the Constitution's equal protection rulings.

What *Romer* and *Bowers* make clear, then, is that beneath the legal language and constitutional terminology of Supreme Court cases lie basic moral and political questions. The Supreme Court is not therefore like the criminal courts, whose task is simply to apply the letter of the law to a given set of facts. It is rather a Court which must sometimes decide the most profound political questions of the day – and decide them as much with reference to moral and political philosophy as to law itself. Difficult and politically risky as this often is, it is also true that most Americans have come to expect the Court to play this role.

The Supreme Court's permanent agenda

Thus far in this chapter we have concentrated upon the great political issues that are tackled by the Court. And we have stressed the fact that the substance of these issues varies over time.

It is important to understand, however, that there are certain kinds of issues which are permanent features of the Supreme Court's agenda. These are issues which arise from the division of governmental powers within the Constitution and which usually pitch one branch of government against another. Unlike the socio-political issues analysed above, these disputes rarely cause great public interest. Nevertheless, they are of great importance because they may directly affect the way in which the the United States is governed.

A useful way to characterise these kinds of cases is that they involve 'intra-governmental' conflicts rather that disputes between government and citizens. This is not to say that they do not involve citizens at all, but rather than their primary importance is how they affect the relative powers of different branches and levels of American government. Let us now look at a few such cases in order to illustrate their nature and significance.

Congress and President

The Constitution deliberately created tensions between congressional and presidential power, and, from time to time, these tensions produce a major dispute which winds up in the Supreme Court. Two cases from the 1980s indicate the technical but important nature of such constitutional questions for the functioning of government.

The budget battle

One of the enduring features of contemporary US politics is the annual wrangling over the budget. Successive Presidents and Congress have long agreed on the need to end budget deficits, but they have rarely been able to agree on which spending programmes should be cut. The result has often been a stalemate and, sometimes, as in 1995, the temporary shutdown of government due to a lack of funds.

In 1985, however, a solution had appeared to have been found. Congress passed, and President Reagan signed, the Balanced Budget and Emergency Deficit Control Act, more commonly known as the Gramm-Rudman Act. The Act provided that when the President and Congress failed to agree on measures to achieve a specified level of deficit reduction, the Comptroller General was empowered to determine the necessary cuts.

This satisfactory political solution to a major governmental problem created a constitutional problem, however. In *Bowsher v. Synar* (1986) the Supreme Court ruled 7 to 2 that the provision was unconstitutional on the grounds that while making budget cuts was an executive power, the Comptroller General was an officer of the legislative branch. To give the Comptroller power to make cuts was thus a violation of the principle of separation of powers.

The legislative veto

Three years before *Bowsher*, the Court had struck down another political compromise designed to facilitate executive–legislative relations. In 1932 Congress had invented the so-called 'legislative veto'. This was a device by which Congress could make a grant of power to the presidency, but retain the right for either the House or the Senate to nullify its use in particular instances.

The legislative veto became a familiar feature of American politics, with over 200 in operation by the 1980s, affecting a wide range of policy areas. Typically, the legislative veto was used to permit Congress to overturn specific decisions promulgated by federal administrative agencies located within the Executive Branch. An example came when the Immigration and Naturalization Service (INS) agreed to allow an overseas student, Jagdish Chadha, to remain in the United States after his student visa had expired. Sometime later, the House of Representatives 'vetoed' this decision.

In *INS v. Chadha* (1983), the Court concluded by a 7–2 vote that the legislative veto was unconstitutional. The Court ruled that the veto was, in effect, a legislative act and yet it did not conform to the constitutionally prescribed procedures for legislating: passage of an identical bill by both houses and signature by the President. The legislative veto was thus an improper use of power by Congress.

Federalism and the commerce power

We noted above that issues of federalism – the division of powers between the States and the federal government – provided some important cases for the Court in its early years. Today such cases are relatively infrequent, as the Court has tended to leave conflicts between Congress and the States to the political process for resolution. However, federalism disputes can still cause American government, and the Court itself, some difficulty.

This is certainly the case where the relative powers of the States and Congress under the Commerce clause are concerned. Article I, section 8 of the Constitution gives Congress the power to regulate commerce between the States, or 'interstate commerce', as it is more commonly known. For many years, the Supreme Court insisted on a fairly clear distinction between *inter*state commerce and *intra*state commerce – business carried on mainly or exclusively within a given State.

With the advent of the New Deal in the 1930s, Congress took increasing control of all forms of commerce and the Supreme Court eventually yielded to this political dynamic. It allowed such a wide definition of interstate commerce that almost no local economic activity seemed off-bounds to congressional regulation.

This trend was compounded in the 1960s when the Court allowed Congress to legislate on non-economic matters in the name of the Commerce clause. Thus, the Court upheld the constitutionality of the 1964 Civil Rights Act on the grounds that local racial discrimination had a negative impact upon interstate commerce (*Heart of Atlanta Motel v. US* and *Katzenbach v. McClung*, both 1964).

It seemed that the original distinctions intended between interstate and intrastate commerce had been virtually obliterated from the Constitution. Then in 1976 the Court surprised everyone with its decision in *National League of Cities v. Usery*. By a vote of 5 to 4, the Justices struck down a 1974 statute that applied federal maximum hours and minimum wages standards to state and municipal government employees. In its Opinion, the Court also drew up some guidelines as to where the Tenth Amendment rights of the States defeated any Commerce clause claims of the Congress.

This attempt to breathe new life into federalism proved so complex and unworkable, however, that in *Garcia v. San Antonio* (1985), the Court actually reversed its position and overruled *National League of Cities*. The Court held that it could not after all satisfactorily draw a clear line between State and federal powers under the Commerce clause. Furthermore, since the States were explicitly represented in the Senate, it would be better to leave the matter to be settled in the legislative arena, where appropriate bargaining could take place.

As recently as 1995, however, the Court again pulled off a surprise. In *US v. Lopez*, the Court ruled that Congress did not possess the power under the Commerce clause to ban the carrying of guns in the proximity of schools. In declaring unconstitutional the Gun-Free School Zones Act of 1990, a 5–4 majority of the Justices rejected the Clinton administration's claim that there was a substantial relationship between possessing a gun in school zones and interstate commerce. The government argued that such gun-carrying adversely affects education and that damaged education means a citizenry less able to serve commerce. The Court did not find that credible, however, and said that if the government's arguments were accepted, 'it is difficult to perceive any limitation on federal power, even in areas such as criminal law enforcement or education where States have historically been sovereign'.

It is not clear whether *Lopez* will prove to be an isolated case or whether it heralds a partial rebirth of federalism. It does serve to illustrate, however, that the Supreme Court always has the potential to alter to some degree the balance of power between the States and the federal government.

Summary

This rather brief review of the contemporary agenda of the Supreme Court necessarily leaves out many important issues on which the Supreme Court regularly makes rulings: First Amendment free speech and religious liberties, Fourth Amendment rights against arbitrary police conduct and Fourteenth Amendment gender equality are just some that spring immediately to mind. (Those wishing to discover more about these issues may find useful the Guide to further reading at the end of this book.)

However, it should be clear by now that the Supreme Court is called upon to play a very significant role in some of the great questions of government and politics in the United States. It should also be clear that the Supreme Court of the United States is neither a purely judicial nor a purely political body. Nevertheless, it is by no means clear that the framers of the Constitution intended the Supreme Court to operate in this fashion. In fact, an examination of the origins of the Supreme Court graphically demonstrates just how much the Court has changed over the past 200 years.

Notes

1 H. Perry, *Deciding to Decide: Agenda Setting in the United States Supreme Court*, Cambridge, Mass., 1991, p. 128.
2 C. Wolfe, *The Rise of Modern Judicial Review*, New York, 1986, p. 259.
3 J. Ely, 'The Wages of Crying Wolf: A Comment on *Roe v. Wade*', *Yale Law Journal*, 1973, pp. 920–49, LXXXll, p. 947.
4 R. Schwed, *Abolition and Capital Punishment*, New York, 1983, p. 103.
5 F. Zimring and G. Hawkins, *Capital Punishment and the American Agenda*, Cambridge, 1986, p. 39.
6 F. Parker, '*Shaw v. Reno*: A Constitutional Setback for Minority Representation', *PS: Political Science and Politics*, March 1995, pp. 47–9, at p. 47.
7 The relevant cases were *Cantwell v. Connecticut* (1940) and *Everson v. Board of Education* (1947), respectively.
8 For sources and a more detailed discussion of American religiosity, see R. McKeever, *Raw Judicial Power? The Supreme Court and American Society* (2nd edn), Manchester, UK, 1995, pp. 245–63, 305–9.

Two—A historical overview

Like other governmental institutions in the United States, the Supreme
Court has evolved considerably in the years since 1789. Indeed, scholars
still debate today what the framers of the Constitution originally
intended the nature and role of the Court to be. As a result, there is
sharp disagreement over whether the Court has transgressed the proper
boundaries of its power. It is important, therefore, to understand the ideas
that underpinned the creation of the Supreme Court in the first place and
how and why it has changed over the years.

Ambiguous beginnings

The origins of the United States Supreme Court are infuriatingly
vague and ambiguous. We know, of course, that the framers of the
Constitution intended to create a supreme court at the head of the
judicial branch of the federal government: but exactly what kind of
court, they did not make fully clear. Most puzzling of all, they gave
no indication in the written text of the Constitution that the Supreme
Court possessed the power of judicial review; and especially they did
not state that it possessed the power to declare acts of Congress unconstitutional. In other words, what we know today as the principal powers of the Supreme Court are nowhere to be found in the Constitution.

Historians have therefore had to scour other sources in an attempt
to ascertain exactly what the framers had in mind when they invented
the Supreme Court. They have, for example, examined the records of
the discussions at the Philadelphia convention of 1787 to see what the
delegates said about judicial review. Unfortunately, those records do
not clarify the position. In the first place, there was relatively little discussion of the Court or of the power of judicial review. Moreover, such
discussion as did take place makes clear only that the framers were
divided over the powers of the Court.[1]

Historians have also looked to the powers exercised by courts in
America in the eighteenth century to see if judicial review was so com-

mon that the framers might simply have assumed that the Supreme
Court would also possess it. Again, however, the record is a mixed one.
In some States, courts had declared state laws unconstitutional, but in
others the practice of judicial review was unknown.

The inescapable conclusion is that the framers had no clear and
agreed view of what the role of the Supreme Court should be. In consequence, the Constitution left the matter vague and open to further
development. We do know, however, that some of the leading cham-
pions of the Constitution of 1787 were ardent supporters of judicial
review. This became evident during the debates over ratification of the
new Constitution.

Alexander Hamilton and judicial review

After the Philadelphia convention concluded in 1787, the campaign for
– and against – ratification of the new Constitution began. In New
York, a series of anonymous newspaper articles were published
explaining the Constitution and urging voters to ratify it. These articles became known collectively as *The Federalist Papers* and were in
fact written by three of the leading delegates at Philadelphia – James
Madison, Alexander Hamilton and John Jay.

In no. 78 of the *Federalist Papers*, Alexander Hamilton gave a
detailed justification not merely of the design of the judicial branch of
the proposed new government but also of the power of judicial review.
The starting point of his argument was the unexceptional observation
that the Constitution was the supreme law of the land. Indeed Article
VI of the Constitution says as much in the so-called 'Supremacy
clause'. Hamilton then proceeded logically to assert that 'no legislative
act, therefore, contrary to the constitution, can be valid'. It is axiomatic
that in a country governed by a constitution, all government acts must
conform to it, since otherwise there is no point in having a constitution at all.

So far, so good. But the next stage of Hamilton's argument is the
problematic one. *Who* is to decide when a legislative act conflicts with
the Constitution and is therefore invalid? This, as we have seen above,
is a matter on which the Constitution is silent. Hamilton, however,
argued that logic required the Supreme Court to be allocated the task
of interpreting the Constitution and, therefore, the right to declare legislative acts void when they are deemed to conflict with it.

Hamilton dismissed the argument that legislatures themselves should be the judge of the constitutionality of their own actions. For this would allow them to substitute their own will for the command of the Constitution. He then wrote:

> It is far more rational to suppose that the Courts were designed to be an intermediate body between the people and the legislature, in order, among other things, to keep the latter within the limits assigned to their authority. The interpretation of the laws is the proper and peculiar province of the courts. A constitution is, in fact, and must be, regarded by judges as a fundamental law. It must therefore belong to them to ascertain its meaning , as well as the meaning of any particular act proceeding from the legislative body. If there should happen to be an irreconcilable variance between the two, that which has the superior obligation and validity ought, of course, to be preferred; in other words, the constitution ought to be preferred to the statute, the intention of the people to the intention of their agents.

Thus did Hamilton argue that *constitutional* supremacy inevitably required *judicial* supremacy. Yet as he himself acknowledged, the notion of judicial supremacy in constitutional interpretation conjured up the possibility that the unelected judiciary might be a more powerful branch of government than the elected Congress. After all, in his scheme, the Supreme Court would have the final word on the validity of acts of Congress.

In another frequently quoted passage, however, Hamilton asserted that there was little to fear from granting the Supreme Court the power of judicial review. For the Court would surely prove to be 'the least dangerous branch' of the national government, that is, the least powerful and therefore the least dangerous in terms of abusing its power to the detriment of the Constitution:

> The executive not only dispenses the honours, but holds the sword of the community: The legislature not only commands the purse, but prescribes the rules by which the duties and rights of every citizen are to be regulated: The judiciary, on the contrary, has no influence over either the sword or the purse; no direction either of the strength or of the wealth of society; and can take no active resolution whatsoever. It may truly be said to have neither FORCE nor WILL, but merely judgement; and must ultimately depend upon the aid of the executive arm for the efficacious exercise of even this faculty.

This key passage added two further justifications for judicial review. First, that because the judiciary was weaker than the Congress and the presidency, the courts could be better entrusted with the power to oversee the actions of other branches of government. Second, the nature of judicial power made it the appropriate place to vest the authority to interpet and apply the Constitution. For in Hamilton's terms, the judiciary exercised 'neither FORCE nor WILL, but merely judgement'. In other words, judicial pronouncements on the meaning of the Constitution would not be coloured by majority opinion or political viewpoint, but merely by neutral judgment. The Court would thus be more objective in interpreting the Constitution than either the legislature or the executive.

We will take up this issue of judicial objectivity in Chapter Four. Suffice it to say at this point that Hamilton's arguments seem highly logical and persuasive. Yet even when the Constitution as a whole was approved, judicial review was still by no means universally accepted. The more democratically-minded politicians of the age feared the power of an unelected judiciary which, they assumed, would ally itself with the wealthy, aristocratically-minded class. Thus, even when Congress enacted detailed legislation on the national judicial structure in the Judiciary Act of 1789, there was again no mention of judicial review. Furthermore when the Jeffersonian Republicans took power following the elections of 1800, they made it very clear that they did not accept judicial supremacy and that each branch of government was the judge of the constitutionality of its own actions.

The failure explicitly to authorise the power of judicial review, either in the Constitution or in the Judiciary Act of 1789, meant that the Supreme Court began its life as an institution with uncertain authority and relatively little prestige. Congress did not bother to supply a new building for the Court and some Americans of note declined an invitation to become a member. Moreover, one of the first Justices of the Supreme Court, John Rutledge, confirmed its low prestige by resigning his seat in 1791 in order to become Chief Justice of the South Carolina Court of Common Pleas.

Marbury v. Madison (1803)

What transformed the prestige, power and role of the Supreme Court in American government was the opinion of Chief Justice John Marshall in *Marbury v. Madison* (1803). For what Congress felt unable to confer on the Court – judicial review – the Justices seized for themselves in this landmark case.

Given that judicial review had always been a political bone of contention between conservatives and radicals, it was appropriate that the

Marbury case should arise from that very conflict. The conservative Federalists had lost the presidential and congressional elections of 1800 to the more democratic Jeffersonian Republicans. In those days, however, a new administration did not take office until March of the following year. The outgoing President John Adams, having lost control of the legislative and executive branches, determined to use this delay to entrench Federalist power in the judicial branch. Most significantly, he appointed his Secretary of State, John Marshall, as Chief Justice of the Supreme Court.

He also created a number of new federal judgeships and filled them with Federalists. One of these was a new Justice of the Peace in the District of Columbia, William Marbury. Unfortunately, the signed commission of Marbury and some other new judges had not been actually delivered by midnight on the last day in office of the Adams administration. The new Secretary of State, James Madison, decided not to complete the appointment of the 'midnight judges', whereupon William Marbury asked the Supreme Court to order Madison to deliver his commission. Thus began the case of *Marbury v. Madison*.

The prime legal issue raised in the case was Marbury's claim that section 13 of the Judiciary Act of 1789 had given the Supreme Court the power to issue a writ of mandamus ordering Madison to deliver his commission. Far more important, however, was the political context and possible consequences of the case. Marbury was asking a *Federalist* Court to compel a *Republican* administration to complete the appointment of a *Federalist* judge. Given the bitter relations between Federalists and Republicans that had developed since the late 1790s, this was political dynamite.

Chief Justice Marshall knew that if he simply ordered Secretary of State Madison to deliver the commission, the order would be contemptuously ignored: the Jefferson administration had already made that much clear when the case first arose. And if that happened, the Court would be seen as politically weak and in no position to advance Federalist designs. If, on the other hand, the Court ruled in favour of Madison, it would surely be seen as having given in to Republican bullying and hence still too weak to act as a source of Federalist power. Either way, the Court looked set for political humiliation.

In the manner of a chess player sacrificing a pawn for a greater advantage later in the game, Marshall and his colleagues manufactured a stunning victory in its decision. For having claimed that Marbury was morally entitled to his judgeship, Marshall said that the Court did

not, however, possess the power to issue the writ of mandamus to
Madison.

Somewhat implausibly manipulating the legal technicalities, Marshall said that section 13 of the Judiciary Act of 1789 was in conflict
with the Constitution. This was because it enlarged the original jurisdiction of the Court as set out in the Constitution: in effect, said Marshall, the Judiciary Act had changed the Constitution. But since one
could only change the Constitution by the process of constitutional
amendment, section 13's grant of the power of mandamus was imper-
missible. The great significance of this was that in the process of
determining Marbury's rights, the Court had for the first time declared
a law unconstitutional and claimed the power of judicial review.

Few scholars doubt that Marshall could have, or even should have,
avoided the entire issue of the constitutionality of section 13. He chose
to focus on it, then, because it allowed him to snatch political victory
from the jaws of defeat. It was brilliantly astute because it gave the Jef-
fersonians what they wanted as far as the midnight judges were concerned. And although some of them railed against Marshall's claim
that the Court had the power to declare an act of Congress unconstitutional, their victory removed the need for a frontal assault on the
Court. Judicial review thus remained on the judicial books as a precedent that could be wheeled out later – and over far more important
issues that a few low-level judicial appointments.

In fact it was to be a further fifty-four years before the Court again
declared an act of Congress unconstitutional. In the meantime, however, the Supreme Court under Marshall employed judicial review to
further the Federalist agenda of strengthening both the national government against the States and national commerce against local regulation. And in so doing, the Court simultaneously enhanced its own
power and prestige within the American political system. In many
respects, therefore, *Marbury v. Madison* was the making of the
Supreme Court.

Consolidation of the Court's power

One the major achievements of the Marshall Court (1801–35) was to
confirm the supremacy of federal law over state law. This was first
achieved in *US v. Peters* (1809), when the Supreme Court decided that
the Pennsylvania legislature could not prevent the enforcement of a
federal law.

The following year, the Court for the first time declared a state law to be unconstitutional. *Fletcher v. Peck* (1810) arose out of the Yazoo Land Fraud in Georgia in the 1790s. The state legislature had corruptly sold land, but in 1796 a reformed legislature had rescinded the sale. An innocent purchaser of the corruptly-sold land challenged the rescinding act as a violation of the Contracts clause of the Constitution (Article I, section 10). The Marshall Court upheld the challenge, thereby striking a triple blow for Federalist philosophy. State laws were declared inferior to the Constitution; the Supreme Court expanded its reach; and property rights were given heightened protection, even in the face of gross political corruption.

Another landmark in the consolidation of the Court's power came in *Martin v. Hunter's Lessee* (1816). Arising out of a legal wrangle over the confiscation of Loyalist lands in Virginia during the War of Independence, the Court was faced with the refusal of the Virginia Supreme Court to implement an earlier US Supreme Court decision affecting the ownership of the lands in dispute. In effect, the Virginia judiciary claimed equal authority to that of the US Supreme Court, even though section 25 of the Judiciary Act of 1789 had explicitly made state Supreme Court decisions reviewable by the Court. In upholding the validity of section 25, the Court reaffirmed its judicial supremacy over the States and state courts in particular.

By this point, the Supreme Court had carved for itself a distinctive and important role in American government. Although it had never explicitly claimed *exclusive* power to interpret the Constitution, it had in fact become the most authoritative arbiter of political and legal disputes in the new nation. This did not mean that the Court was unchallenged: indeed then as now, the Court's power was circumscribed by political realities and the need to accommodate other political forces. Nevertheless, judicial supremacy was now the working principle of American constitutionalism.

As already indicated, judicial supremacy was put to work on behalf of national government power and national commerce. No case was more important in this respect than *McCulloch v. Maryland* (1819). Federalists had long believed that a national bank was a necessary instrument of financial stability. Many Republicans opposed it, however, both because they disputed its necessity and because they believed Congress had no constitutional authority to create such a bank. When the Second Bank of the United States was nevertheless chartered by Congress in 1816 (the First having been allowed to lapse), many States moved to impose taxes on its branch operations within their boundaries. This, in effect, was a challenge to federal sovereignty over the Bank.

The Marshall Court ruled unanimously that Congress had the power to incorporate the Bank and that the States had no power to tax it. What was of enormous significance, however, was Marshall's rationale for these conclusions. He conceded that the federal government was one of limited and enumerated powers and that the power to charter a corporation was not specified in the Constitution.

However, he pointed out that Congress was given the right 'to make all laws which shall be necessary and proper' for exercising the powers which *had* been enumerated. From this 'necessary and proper clause', he evolved the doctrine of 'implied powers' – unspecified powers to enact legislation which advanced the exercise of the specified powers. In short, after *McCulloch*, the Congress was endowed with a much broader legislative power *vis-à-vis* the States than had been claimed before.

Marshall also took the opportunity presented in *McCulloch* to argue that the Constitution was a general statement, rather than a blueprint, and must be interpreted with a degree of flexibility. It was, he said, 'a constitution intended to endure for ages to come, and, consequently, to be adapted to the various crises of human affairs'. Marshall was articulating here the concept of 'the living Constitution', as it is sometimes called. Rather than being immutably fixed in all its aspects, the Constitution is like an organism in its capacity for growth and development. Above all, it must adapt its broad principles to the changing needs of a dynamic society.

Implicitly, the *McCulloch* Opinion also validated a continuing powerful role for the Supreme Court. For if the Constitution required 'adaptation' from time to time, who but the Supreme Court would initiate or sanction the necessary flexibility? In short, 'broad construction' of the Constitution, combined with judicial supremacy, made the Supreme Court an even more vital player in American government and politics, both now and in the future.

The Taney Court (1835–64)

By the time Chief Justice John Marshall retired in 1835, the Court had played a significant part in establishing national authority over the States. In 1828, however, Andrew Jackson had been elected President and, although a dedicated nationalist, he was also a firm believer in States' rights. Jacksonian Democracy also encompassed a dislike of economic privilege combined with support for equal opportunity for the less well-off. Unsurprisingly he chose as Chief Justice a man of similar philosophy, Roger Taney.

The Taney Court moderated some of the Marshall Court's strict protection of private property rights and federal power over the regulation of commerce. An emblematic decision of the Taney Court came in *Charles River Bridge v. Warren Bridge* (1837). In 1785 the State of Massachusetts had contracted for the construction of a bridge across the Charles River from Charleston to Boston. The bridge owners were permitted to collect tolls. In 1828, however, the State authorised the construction of a second bridge, the Warren Bridge, the owners of which would also be allowed to collect tolls. The Charles River Bridge owners argued that they had been given an exclusive contract and that the Warren Bridge was therefore invalid under the Contracts clause of the Constitution.

Justice Story, a longtime ally of Chief Justice Marshall, supported this argument on the grounds of the sanctity of vested property rights. But Taney and the new Jacksonian majority on the Court disagreed. While he acknowledged the importance of property rights, Taney argued that they must sometimes give way before the ultimate purpose of government, which is 'to promote the happiness and prosperity of the community'.

The Taney Court also allowed the States greater powers in commercial regulation, although never at the cost of threatening federal supremacy over interstate commerce. Indeed, perhaps the greatest contrast between the Marshall Court and the Taney Court was that whereas the former issued bold and incisive decisions, the latter employed narrow arguments. Thus while the Marshall Court gained a reputation for judicial activism, the Taney Court generally practised judicial restraint.

A good illustration of this was the Taney Court's invention of the 'political questions' doctrine in *Luther v. Borden* (1849). The case arose from the so-called Dorr Rebellion in Rhode Island. The State's voting register was characterised by gross disfranchisement of urban voters. A reform movement, led by Thomas Dorr, established a rival constitution and government and the Supreme Court was called in to adjudicate which was the proper government of the State. Taney ducked the issue, however, arguing that this was a 'political question' to be settled by the people and the political process, rather than by the judiciary.

The Taney Court was thus cautious and restrained in comparison with the Marshall Court. And the contrast between the two illustrates the extent to which the Justices determine for themselves precisely how and to what extent they employ the judicial power in the governmental process.

That said, the Taney Court is generally remembered not for its characteristic restraint, but for its one great, disastrous foray into activism in *Dred Scott v. Sandford* (1857). In this case the Court pronounced a sweeping vindication of slaveowners' rights throughout the United States and thereby played a major part in bringing on the Civil War. The Taney Court can therefore be viewed both as an example of judicial caution in harmony with the political times, and of dangerous judicial intervention in highly-politicised conflicts.

Taken as a whole, however, the Supreme Court employed judicial review to declare laws unconstitutional relatively infrequently under Marshall and Taney. Between 1803 and 1864, just two federal laws and only forty state laws and local ordinances were declared unconstitutional.[2] While it is important to emphasise that many of these decisions were critical in the establishment of the new system of government and broad national policy, the record also indicates little inclination on the part of the Justices to make the Court a contributor to detailed policy-making. At this point in its history, the Court was more concerned with broad principles than precise policies.

The Supreme Court in the industrial age

Like other governmental institutions, the Supreme Court has developed and changed in tune with the rhythms of American history. Thus when the upheavals of industrialisation hit the United States in the decades following the Civil War, the Supreme Court was deeply affected. It was not merely that industrialisation transformed the agenda of American politics, but also that the very role of government itself was subjected to fundamental re-examination.

In the antebellum period, the culture and practice of American government had not fundamentally altered. Certainly the federal government had expanded its reach in certain policy areas, but public expectations of what government should do remained generally limited to the original concerns of the framers of the Constitution.

These expectations, however, changed rapidly with the onset of industrialisation and its associated social and economic problems. A series of reform movements emerged in the last third of the nineteenth century which demanded both state and federal government action on matters such as trade union rights, wages and hours regulations, health and safety in factories, income tax and the power of the new giant industrial corporations. In short, American government came under increasing pressure to reform and regulate the new industrial society, even though no such expansive role for government was envisaged in the Constitution of 1787.

Inevitably, as the established arbiter of constitutional disputes, the Supreme Court became enmeshed in the political conflict between those who demanded greater governmental activism and those who were determined to resist this transformation. Moreover, the nature of the federal judiciary's intervention in this most fundamental of political cleavages entailed a significant change in the role of the Supreme Court itself in the policy-making process.

At first, the Court was accommodating to the nascent regulatory regime. In *Munn v. Illinois* (1877), for example, the Court upheld the power of States to set the rates charged by grain-elevator operators to farmers. The regulatory statute had resulted from political pressures brought to bear on legislators by farmers who believed they were being charged extortionate rates by operators who made agreements on prices between themselves.

For their part, the operators claimed that the statute was unconstitutional on two major grounds. First, it violated the principle of federalism, since the Constitution assigned the power to make such regulations to Congress rather than the States. Second, it violated the property rights of the operators under the Due Process clause of the Fourteenth Amendment. In a 7–2 vote, however, the Court upheld the regulation. The substance of the Court's decision was based on its view that some businesses, although privately owned, were 'so affected with a public interest' that they ceased to be solely a private matter. Such businesses were therefore subject to reasonable regulation by public authorities.

Moreover, in his Opinion for the Court, Chief Justice Morrison Waite issued what became a classic dictum of judicial restraint: 'For protection against abuses by legislatures, the people must resort to the polls, not the courts.' The *Munn* Court thus combined a flexible concept of private property with deference to elected legislatures that boded well for future regulatory activity by government.

Substantive due process

However, it was the views of one of the dissenters in Munn, Justice Stephen Field, that eventually captured the Court. Field developed the doctrine that became known as 'substantive due process'. This was based on the belief that the Due Process clause of the Fifth and Four-teenth Amendments protected more than mere process, or the manner in which persons could be deprived of 'life, liberty or property'. In a stunning new interpretation of the clause, Field argued that, in addi-tion, there were actual rights which government could not touch either with or without proper procedures. These rights, although not men-tioned in the Fifth and Fourteenth Amendments, were simply beyond the reach of government in the American political system.

For Field, and soon a majority of his colleagues, the main rights protected by the Due Process clause were economic in nature: in par-ticular, freedom of contract and private property rights. In terms of ideology and policy, Field read *laissez-faire* economics into the Con-stitution. And as the political conflict between defenders of *laissez-faire* and interventionist reformers grew more intense, a majority of the Jus-tices of the Supreme Court came to regard it as their duty to hold back the tide of government intrusion into the realm of economic liberty.

As a consequence, the Court issued a series of major decisions, now regarded as notorious. In 1895, for example, the Court ruled in *US v. E. C. Knight Co.* that the federal government, committed by the Sher-man Antitrust Act to ending monopoly practices, had no power to break up a company that controlled the production of over 90 per cent of all refined sugar in America. The Court based its decision on the assertion that the federal commerce power covered only trade and not production.

Perhaps the Court's most infamous decision of all came in *Lochner v. New York* (1905) when a 5–4 majority of the Justices held that the Due Process clause protected liberty of contract to the extent that it was infringed by a New York statute limiting the hours of bakery workers to ten a day or sixty a week. The Court dismissed the State's claim that the statute was enacted in pursuit of the health and safety of bakery workers, arguing instead that it was simply a violation of the right of both employers and employees to freely negotiate the terms of work.

This unrealistic view of the relative power of employers and employees in contract negotiations was compounded three years later in *Adair v. US* (1908). This declared unconstitutional the federal Erdman Act of 1898, which outlawed so-called 'yellow-dog contracts'. These were contracts of employment which prohibited workers from joining a labour union. Once again, the Court deemed such intervention to be a violation of the freedom of contract of both employers and employees.

The Court, it should be noted, never claimed that freedom of contract or other economic liberties were absolute. Indeed, it occasionally upheld some statutory regulations of terms of employment. However, armed with the weapon of substantive due process, the Court now insisted in effect that all such government regulations satisfy the Justices that the public benefit sought was sufficiently exceptional to override the norm of freedom of contract. In short, substantive due process enabled the Supreme Court to exercise close supervision over socioeconomic policy. For the first time in its history, then, the Court became a major, continuous policy-maker in the American political system.

This new role that the Court had arrogated to itself came under increasing fire as the demand for government reform became more insistent. The main criticism directed at the Court was that the Justices, far from enforcing the clear command of the Constitution, were merely substituting their own political and social views for those of the people's elected representatives. In the minds of these critics, the fears of those who had originally opposed granting the Court the power of judicial review had been realised: the federal judiciary was undermining American democracy by usurping the legitimate policy-making powers of elected legislatures.

Whether this criticism was, in fact, justified is still a matter of debate. It can be argued that the Court was indeed trying to be faithful to the original vision of constitutional economic freedoms, even though that caused tensions in a rapidly changing society. It might also be argued that the increased judicial activism of this era was simply an inevitable by-product of increased governmental activism generally. Whatever the explanation of the Justices' behaviour, however, the fact remains that the Court was acting as a block on the political desires of many Americans. And that fact created a fundamental crisis in American politics when the Great Depression decimated the United States in the 1930s.

The Supreme Court and the New Deal

From the 1890s to the early 1930s, the predominantly conservative jurisprudence of the Court had not been without its supporters in the broader American political system. Indeed, apart from the Progressive Era (1901–17), conservative forces had had the upper hand in electoral politics. The Great Depression, however, brought about an electoral realignment. The Democrats, who had won only two presidential elections between 1896 and 1928, became the dominant party in American politics. More importantly, the new Democrat ascendancy was based on the policies of New Deal Liberalism. These policies were engendered by the need to combat the economic collapse and social deprivation which began with the Wall Street Crash of October 1929 and only came to an end with the onset of World War II in 1939.

New Deal Liberalism was based on the belief that the federal government must take responsibility for the health of the economy and the well-being of the American people. In turn, these new responsibilities required an unprecedented level of government planning, regulation and intervention, particularly on behalf of the less well-off members of society.

Franklin D. Roosevelt was elected president in 1932 on the promise to initiate these bold experiments in government and was overwhelmingly re-elected in 1936. In the same period, the Democrats also achieved great victories in the congressional elections, with the result that numerous New Deal policies were enacted.

Much of this legislation ran counter to the entire thrust of the Supreme Court's jurisprudence over recent decades and inevitably many New Deal measures found themselves under constitutional challenge before the Supreme Court. At first, the *laissez-faire* majority on the Court stayed resolute, particularly the so-called 'Four Horsemen of Reaction' – Justices George Sutherland, James McReynolds, Willis Van Devanter and Pierce Butler. With varying degrees of support from other Justices, this block of Justices struck down many of the key measures of the New Deal, including the National Industrial Recovery Act of 1933 (*Schechter Poultry Corporation v. US*, 1935) and the Agricultural Adjustment Act of 1933 (*US v. Butler*, 1936).

The Court-packing plan

A furious President Roosevelt set out to curb the power of the Court and force it to accept the New Deal. In 1937, he sent the so-called 'Court-packing bill' to Congress. This was a measure that would allow him to appoint an additional Justice to the Court for each current Justice over the age of seventy. Disingenuously presented as a measure to help the Court cope with its arduous workload, it was simply a device by which to create a New Deal majority on the Court: fully six of the nine current members were over seventy!

There was great resistance to the bill, even among Roosevelt's usual supporters. Such a naked attempt to manipulate and subordinate a co-equal branch of the federal government struck many as unhealthy for American democracy. But it was the Court itself which effectively scuppered the bill by backing down from its confrontation with the New Deal. In 1937, in *West Coast Hotel v. Parrish*, the Court upheld a minimum wage law from the State of Washington. What was significant was that the Washington statute was virtually identical to a law which had been struck down as a violation of freedom of contract in 1923, in *Adkins v. Children's Hospital*. In effect, the Court had committed a volte-face. There soon followed a series of decisions making it clear that the Court was abandoning its role as overseer of socio-economic policy and that, henceforth, the federal government would be permitted to do virtually what it liked in this area of policy, no matter what the Constitution appeared to say.

The Court's so-called 'switch-in-time that saved nine' ensured that the court-packing bill would not be passed. However, it showed very clearly the practical limits to the Supreme Court's power and role. Above all, it demonstrated that, isolated from other centres of political power, the Court could not enforce its view of the Constitution against the wishes of the President, the Congress and the American people. In a crisis at least, judicial supremacy over constitutional meaning proved incapable of withstanding sheer political force.

The modern court

As we saw in the previous chapter, the crisis of the 1930s left the Supreme Court with less power and prestige than at any previous point in its history. Not merely had the substance of its decisions attracted the ire of the nation, but constitutional interpretation had been exposed to many outside of the legal profession as fraudulent. Justices who had been claiming to speak in the name of the Constitution were revealed instead as the mouthpieces of a narrow class ideology and interest.

Discredited and forced to retreat, the Court entered a period of passivity and readjustment. Although new crises soon beset the country, in the form of World War II and then the Cold War, the Court made no attempt to influence policy in respect of them. Even when measures aimed at containing enemy influence raised major issues of constitutional rights, the Court fell into line with the lead given by the President and Congress.

The liberal consensus in post-war America called for government intervention in the domestic economy and passionate anti-communism both at home and abroad. The Court under Chief Justices Stone (1941–46) and Vinson (1946–53) lacked either the means or the will to challenge that consensus in the name of the Constitution. The struggle over the New Deal had seemingly deprived the Court of the intellectual and institutional resources necessary to play a major policy-making role in American government.

The Warren Court

It was the genius of the Warren Court to resurrect judicial power, but in a manner which, initially at least, did not threaten the post-war liberal consensus. Instead, the Warren Court embraced that consensus and then carved from it a special area of competence for the federal judiciary. In so doing, the Warren Court devised the platform not merely for a new bout of judicial activism, but also for a new dimension to the Court's governmental role.

The key to the restoration of judicial power under Warren was the return of the Supreme Court to the moral high ground of American politics. This was achieved through the Court's crusade for the recognition of the political and legal equality of black Americans throughout the country and especially in the South. Although the Court's racial equality decisions provoked vehement resistance in the South, the nation's liberal elite and much of the general populace believed that the Court's new activism was right and even courageous. As is usually the case, it was the substance of the Court's decisions which was most important for the great majority of politicians and the public. And along with approval of the Court's civil rights agenda came approval of, or at least indifference to, the return of judicial activism. So long as the Court was perceived as doing good, most Americans saw no threat in the revival of judicial power.

In the 1960s, however, what began as a judicial campaign against racial discrimination gradually expanded into other areas of civil rights and liberties. The net result was that the Court transformed itself into the arbiter of socio-moral conflicts in American society, just as it had earlier claimed the same authority over socio-economic conflicts. Where the Court had once dictated the details of wage and price legislation or congressional regulation of agriculture and industry, the Warren Court and then the Burger Court now engaged in active oversight of policy on matters such as race and gender equality, contraception and abortion, religious activities in public schools and the rights of producers and consumers of obscene and pornographic materials.

Moreover, unlike earlier Courts, the Warren and Burger Courts did not confine themselves to telling other branches of government what they could not do. At times, they also instructed government officials on what they must do by way of duties and positive responsibilities towards certain groups and individuals. Thus the Court in the 1960s and 1970s engaged not merely in activism, but in affirmative activism.

In some respects, the Court was encouraged to play this more active and detailed role in policy-making. Members of Congress, for example, often found it convenient to leave the Court to take the lead on controversial issues and policies, since this permitted them to escape the pressures generated by social conflicts. And on other occasions, when Congress found itself unable to agree on policy details, it happily left the Court to solve the difficulties it lacked the political will to address.

Unsurprisingly, many commentators noted that the Court had acquired a new role in American policy-making and government. Nathan Glazer considered that the United States now had an 'imperial judiciary',[3] whose ambition was not confined to particular ideological goals but which seemed to seek power for its own sake. Vincent Blasi similarly noted a 'rootless activism'[4] in the work of the Burger Court, while Donald Horowitz concluded that there was a new tendency in American government 'to commit the resolution of social policy issues to the courts'.[5]

Unfortunately for the Justices, the liberal consensus which originally underpinned the Warren and Burger Courts' activism did not extend into all areas of public policy. And when social issues became major sources of political conflict in the late 1960s and early 1970s, so too did the Court's decisions and the judicial activism which advanced them. Almost inevitably, then, the new role of the Court came under attack from conservative politicians who deplored the Court's generally liberal decisions. They raised the old cry of judicial usurpation of the proper powers of the people's elected representatives and so once again, judicial activism was charged with undermining American democracy.

By the end of the 1980s, the efforts of the Reagan and Bush administrations had paid off to the extent that the Court was now modifying some of its earlier decisions in a more conservative direction and refusing to take any bold initiatives. In other words, a familiar pattern of cyclical activism and restraint, conservatism and liberalism seemed to be asserting itself. In the twentieth century, the Court has moved from conservative activism to liberal restraint and then to liberal activism followed by conservative restraint.

Summary

Two things seem clear from this brief history of the Court's role in American government. First, that the Court has no precisely fixed role. This stems originally from the failure of the framers of the Constitution to specify the powers of the Supreme Court and the functions of the judiciary in a constitutional democracy.

Second, it follows that the Court is free to develop its own role and powers, subject, however, to the consent or acquiescence of the other branches of government. If the Court arouses too much hostility in those branches, it will surely come under attack and will be forced to retreat. It is worth emphasising, however, that what arouses the hostility of the other branches of government is less the self-proclaimed role of the Court at any particular moment in history, and more the actual substance of the policies that this role generates. Thus it is not so much the Court's role that tends to make political enemies – it is the Court's decisions.

Despite the undoubted involvement of the Supreme Court in politics, however, it is important not to forget that it remains, in key respects, a court composed of judges. Let us now turn then to a consideration of the Court's major legal and judicial dimensions.

Notes

1 R. Carr, *The Supreme Court and Judicial Review*, New York, 1942, pp.45–6.
2 L. Epstein, J. Segal, H. Spaeth and T. Walker, *The Supreme Court Compendium: Data, Decisions, and Development*, Washington, D.C., 1994.

3 N. Glazer, 'Toward an Imperial Judiciary', *The Public Interest*, XLI, 1975, pp. 104–23.
4 V. Blasi, 'The Rootless Activism of the Burger Court', in V. Blasi (ed.), *The Burger Court: The Counter-Revolution That Wasn't*, New Haven, 1983, pp. 198–217.
5 D. Horowitz, The Courts and Social Policy, Washington, D.C., 1977, p. 12.

Three—Cases, decisions and judicial procedures

One of the most important facts about the power of the Supreme Court is that it cannot simply take up any issue it wishes. Rather, it must wait for someone to file a suit in a lower court and then for that case to be reviewed by intermediate courts. Only then does the Supreme Court have the power to choose which cases it will hear. Moreover, the way the Court deals with cases is governed by certain judicial and legal criteria and procedures which shape the ultimate decisions it makes.

The personal is political ... and legal

Supreme Court cases have a somewhat austere and forbidding facade of judicial procedure and language. Yet behind this, there is often a fascinating and stirring personal story which provides the context for judicial decisions of great political significance. This is particularly true of cases involving questions of civil liberties. In these cases, one person's struggle or grievance can become the catalyst for great judicial debates about political powers and rights. By looking at some examples in detail, we can see the process by which the personal, the judicial and the political are interwoven in some of the Court's most important cases.

Clarence Gideon's story

Clarence Earl Gideon was an unlikely character to figure in the civil liberties 'Hall of Fame'. Ill-educated and semi-literate, he pursued a life of petty crime in his home State of Florida, usually unsuccessfully. One description of him read:

> Gideon was a fifty-one-year-old white man who had been in and out of prisons much of his life. He had served time for four previous felonies, and he bore the physical marks of a destitute life: a wrinkled, prematurely aged face, a voice and hands that trembled, a frail body, white hair. He had never been a professional criminal or a man of violence; he just could not

seem to settle down to work, and so he made his way by gambling and occasional thefts.[1]

In line with this background, Gideon was arrested in 1961 charged with breaking and entering a poolroom. This was a felony, or serious crime, under Florida law and was punishable by imprisonment.

Apart from the charge itself, Gideon faced a major problem common to many small time criminals: he was too poor to hire a lawyer to defend himself. Without the expert advice of legal counsel, it would be difficult enough for him to understand the judicial procedures that would decide his fate, let alone be able to mount an effective defence. Gideon understood this well enough and asked the trial court to appoint and pay for a lawyer on his behalf. The court, however, refused. Gideon had no alternative but to conduct his own defence and, although he made a decent attempt under the circumstances, he was found guilty and sentenced to prison.

Most people in his position would have given up at this point. Gideon, however, having now learned a little law, made an appeal to the Florida Supreme Court. He claimed that by not providing him with defence counsel, Florida had denied him a fair trial. As such, the State had violated the Fourteenth Amendment of the United States Constitution, which says that no State shall 'deprive any person of life, liberty, or property, without due process of law'. The issue for decision, then, was whether the requirements of 'due process' included not merely the right of the accused to employ a defence lawyer if he could afford one, but also the duty of the State to provide a defence lawyer if the accused was indigent (poor).

Unfortunately for Clarence Gideon, the Florida Supreme Court rejected his appeal. It pointed to the decision of the United States Supreme Court in *Betts v. Brady* (1942), which said that States only had a duty to provide defence counsel for indigents in very exceptional circumstances. Since Gideon's case was anything but exceptional, provision of counsel was not necessary to assure him of a fair trial and 'due process'.

The Florida Supreme Court had clearly stated the correct constitutional position as it stood. Nevertheless, the determined Gideon decided to appeal to the US Supreme Court – the highest court in the land. He would ask the Supreme Court to overrule its earlier decision in *Betts v. Brady*, and thus interpret the Fourteenth Amendment's due process clause in a new way – to require the provision of defence counsel for indigents accused of serious crimes.

At this point, the discretion of the US Supreme Court came into play. It had two fundamental decisions to make. The first was whether to entertain Gideon's appeal at all. If it so wished, the Court could simply dismiss the appeal, citing the *Betts* precedent as controlling. However, if it did decide to review the Florida court's decision, there was still the second and far more important decision to make: should the Court overturn a constitutional ruling it had made just twenty years before and order Florida and other States to provide counsel for indigents?

The decisions facing the Court were problematic for a number of reasons. On the one hand, there was a strong argument which said that, given the complexities of the legal process, a person could not be guaranteed a fair trial unless represented by expert counsel. Indeed, even at the time of the *Betts* case in 1942, some thirty-five States had adopted precisely that position and had enacted legislation requiring the provision of counsel for indigents in felony cases.

On the other hand, Florida was one of those States which had chosen not to do so, and the constitutional principle of federalism appeared to leave this decision in the hands of States, rather than the federal authorities. Moreover, not so long ago the Supreme Court itself had explicitly upheld the distinction between trials in state courts and trials in federal courts. In 1938, in *Johnson v. Zerbst*, the Court had considered the meaning of the Sixth Amendment, which said that 'In all criminal prosecutions, the accused shall enjoy the right ... to have the Assistance of Counsel for his defence.' In concluding that this required the provision of counsel for the poor, the Court, however, also reiterated the standard view that the Sixth Amendment applied only to federal trials, not state trials. It reinforced this distinction just four years later in *Betts*, as we have seen.

For Clarence Gideon to win his appeal, therefore, the Supreme Court would have to argue for a departure from the original meaning of the Sixth and Fourteenth Amendments and from the controlling power of recent precedent. While the Court has never felt itself absolutely bound by its own prior decisions, it has always held that respect for precedent and the need for stability in the law are crucial elements of judicial decision-making.

Despite these difficulties, however, the Supreme Court ruled unanimously (9–0) in Clarence Gideon's favour. Moreover, the decision in *Gideon v. Wainwright* (1963) was only the beginning of a radical change in the law of the Constitution on the right to counsel. Today, indigents accused of less serious crimes than felonies also have the right to be provided with counsel. Indeed, even suspects not yet formally accused must be provided with counsel. As a result, many cities and some States have created Public Defenders Offices to deal specifically with the needs of the indigent accused. In other areas, trial courts appoint private lawyers to do this work. *Gideon v. Wainwright* was very important then, not only for Clarence Gideon, but for all those indigent Americans suspected or accused of criminal offences.

And what of Clarence Gideon himself? Winning his case before the Supreme Court did not mean automatic acquittal on the breaking and entering charge. Rather, he had won the right to a re-trial. This time, however, he had the assistance of counsel. With this help, new witnesses were found and the testimony of the prosecution's witnesses from the first trial was discredited. Clarence Gideon was found 'not guilty'.

Dred Scott's story

The case in which the slave Dred Scott became entangled before the Civil War (1861–5) is the most infamous in the history of the Supreme Court. What began as Scott's fairly routine and uncontroversial attempt to be declared a free man became a bitter source of political conflict and resulted in a disastrous decision by the Court that helped to precipitate the Civil War.

Scott was owned by an army surgeon, John Emerson, whose work took him and his slaves to various parts of the country. As a result, Scott had lived in Illinois and the Wisconsin Territory, both areas in which slavery was banned. When his owner died in 1843, Scott was resident in Missouri, a State which permitted slavery. Three years later, and with the blessing of Emerson's widow, Scott and his wife Harriet filed suit in a Missouri court, asking to be declared free. Despite the fact that Missouri was still a slave State, the basic legal issue was largely unproblematic: by having lived in free territory, Scott stood to benefit from the legal maxim operative in Missouri of 'once free, always free'. Sure enough, in 1850, the Missouri court ordered Scott and his wife freed.

It was only at this point that difficulties arose. By 1850, Mrs Emerson had left Missouri and placed her financial affairs there in the hands of her brother, John Sanford. He was now obliged to pay Scott wages dating back to the first court hearing of the case in 1847. Rather than do so, however, he appealed the decision to free Scott to the Missouri Supreme Court.

In the years since Scott had first filed suit, the issue of slavery had become more bitterly contested than ever before. The so-called Great Compromise of 1850 was but the latest attempt to resolve the issue, but it did nothing to quell the underlying passions that fuelled the controversy. By the time Sanford's appeal came before the Missouri Supreme Court in 1852, his lawyer was able to employ pro-slavery and States' Rights rhetoric to considerable effect. The Missouri Supreme Court reversed the lower court and the precedent of 'once free, always free'.

For technical reasons of legal strategy, Scott's lawyers did not simply appeal this decision directly to the United States Supreme Court. Rather they began a new suit which raised substantially the same issues. This was the case of *Dred Scott v. Sandford* (Sanford's name was misspelt in the records).

In 1857, the United States Supreme Court announced its decision. By a 7–2 majority, the Justices made a series of pronouncements that dealt a devastating blow to Scott and, indeed, to the whole anti-slavery movement. Amongst other things, the Court declared first, that a slave was not a United States citizen and therefore was not entitled to bring suit in a federal court. Second, Congress did not have the power to ban slavery in Territories, such as Wisconsin where Scott had lived. And third, although Illinois did have the right to ban slavery within its own boundaries, once Scott had voluntarily returned to Missouri, a slave State, he automatically reverted to slave status. Finally, the Court said, slaves were their owners' property and the United States Constitution protected owners' property rights throughout the United States.

The decision in *Dred Scott v. Sandford* was, with some justification, viewed as motivated by the pro-slavery sentiments of the Court's majority. While the pro-slavery South rejoiced therefore, anti-slavery activists and politicians had no intention of respecting the decision and thus the Court's authority. Indeed, the *Dred Scott* case convinced many that compromise with the South on slavery was no longer possible. In that sense, the decision helped propel the country towards civil war in 1861.

Slavery was abolished in 1865, when the Thirteenth Amendment to the Constitution was ratified following the military defeat of the South. For Dred Scott, unfortunately, it came too late. He died in 1858, having never won the freedom that had seemed certain to be his back when he started his suit in 1846. Nevertheless, by taking his cause to the United States Supreme Court, Scott had played a significant part in bringing the conflict over slavery to a climax and slavery itself to an end.

Jane Roe's story

Jane Roe was the pseudonym adopted by a young Texan woman, Norma McCorvey, when she provided the test case for abortion rights in 1970. McCorvey's life up to that point had not been a great success. She had dropped out of high school, was divorced with a young child and had few career prospects. When she became pregnant in 1969, she sought an abortion.

However, under Texas law, abortion was only permitted when necessary to save the mother's life, so McCorvey was faced with the choice of an illegal 'back street' abortion or giving birth. She chose the latter and the resulting child was put up for adoption. Many other women throughout history had faced the same dilemma and that might have been the end of this particular episode.

But Norma McCorvey lived in a time of great social change, change which included a new wave of the women's movement. All over America, women were demanding equality with men and part of their campaign was for 'reproductive freedom'. Many women believed that until they were able to control their own fertility through easy access to contraception and abortion, they would always be held back in their careers by the demands of motherhood. Two such women, Sarah Weddington and Linda Coffee, were lawyers planning to challenge the constitutionality of restrictive state abortion laws before the United States Supreme Court. Hearing of McCorvey's experience, they approached her and eventually asked her to provide the test case for a challenge to the Texas abortion statute. She agreed and in 1970, Jane Roe filed suit in a federal district court in Texas against the Dallas County District Attorney, Henry Wade. The historic case of *Roe v. Wade* had begun.

The heart of Jane Roe's argument was that the Texas abortion statute violated her constitutional right to privacy. Although no such right was mentioned in the text of the Constitution, the Supreme Court had ruled in *Griswold v. Connecticut* (1965) that a right to privacy could be inferred from various clauses in that document. In *Gris-*

wold the Court had ruled that this covered a married couple's right to use contraceptives, something banned in Connecticut. Then, in *Eisenstadt v. Baird* (1971), the Court had extended the right to use contraceptives to all adults, married or not. Now Jane Roe's case was to press that the *Griswold* privacy right be further extended, this time to allow a pregnant woman to decide whether or not she wanted an abortion.

The essence of the State's case was that there was no constitutional right to privacy and no fundamental right of a woman to have an abortion. On the contrary, the State had a compelling interest in protecting the potential life of the unborn fetus or embryo and that was what its abortion statute sought to accomplish. Moreover, the constitutional principle of federalism had always been applied to the issue of abortion, meaning that States rather than the federal government had the power to determine abortion policy.

The federal district court decided that Jane Roe did have a constitutional right to an abortion; but for technical reasons, the court did not order Texas to stop enforcing its law against other women. Both Roe and Texas, therefore, decided to appeal to the Supreme Court. In 1973, the Justices voted 7–2 to uphold Jane Roe's claim and declared the Texas statute unconstitutional and unenforceable. A woman, said the Supreme Court, has a fundamental constitutional right to decide for herself whether or not to have a child. This included the right to choose an abortion. As the case had been filed as a so-called 'class action', all women in Texas had the same right to an abortion as, by implication, did all women throughout the United States.

The Court's decision was highly controversial. Of course, abortion is a very emotive issue and any pronouncement upon it is likely to cause conflict. But there was more to criticism of the Court's decision than that. The majority Justices were accused of ignoring basic legal and constitutional principles and, in fact, behaving more like legislators than judges.

Thus, for example, critics charged that the Court had ignored the rule of 'standing'. This means that in order to bring a case before the Court, a plaintiff must present a concrete 'case or controversy' as outlined in Article III of the Constitution. Yet even by the time that Roe had brought her case in the federal district court, she was no longer pregnant. The facts which had originally given rise to the case had long since disappeared and this was grounds for declaring it 'moot'. Certainly the Court could have taken this option: but as the majority Justices argued, this would make it extremely difficult for any case involving pregnancy to be litigated given the snail's pace at which the legal process usually moves!

In the substance of its decision, the Court also provoked an outcry by creating a very broad right to abortion. In effect a woman could not be banned from having an abortion during the first six months of pregnancy. Even in the final three months, States could not prohibit abortions if continuing the pregnancy seriously threatened the mother's health or life.

For those who believe in a woman's 'right to choose' an abortion, *Roe v. Wade* was a great victory. Quite simply, provided she took steps within the first six months of pregnancy, never again would a woman be legally compelled to have a child that she did not want. For opponents, however – those who believe in a 'right to life' – the *Roe* decision was akin to approving the murder of 'innocent children'.

As we have already noted, however, none of this was of benefit to Norma McCorvey. She had played a vital role in a Supreme Court ruling that has affected the lives of millions of American women since 1973, even though she could not personally avail herself of the *Roe* abortion right.

In fact, Norma McCorvey has not found it easy to come to terms with the role she played. In the 1980s she acknowledged that she was indeed Jane Roe and became something of a celebrity in 'pro-choice' circles. In 1995, however, she was baptised a Christian by the Reverend Flip Benham, national director of Operation Rescue. Operation Rescue is the one of the most militant 'pro-life' groups dedicated to stopping abortions and overthrowing *Roe v. Wade*. Norma McCorvey claims she still supports the right to abortion in the first three months of pregnancy, but not thereafter. Perhaps she will change her position again. But however she finally decides, she has already left her mark on American society and the Constitution.

Even the sketches of the three cases discussed above indicate the complex blend of the personal, the political and the legal that is involved in the work of the Supreme Court. Nevertheless, although there is clearly much more to the Court's role in American government than law, the basic fact that needs to be understood is that the Supreme Court was established as *a court*, endowed with *judicial* power.

This means that the personal and political dimensions of issues such as race equality and abortion are channelled into judicial procedures that are, in many respects, typical of courts everywhere. This in turn means that the framework of Supreme Court decision-making is quite different from that of the executive and legislative branches of government. Thus, while the Supreme Court makes public policy on some of the great issues of the day, it must do so within the confines of law suits: and that can make an important difference to the policy that emerges.

Let us now, therefore, examine the formal powers and procedures of the Supreme Court, in order to gain an understanding of how this unique institution operates.

The nation's highest court

The Supreme Court is the highest court in the land. It was created by Article III of the Constitution, which begins: 'The judicial Power of the United States, shall be vested in one supreme Court, and in such inferior Courts as the Congress may from time to time ordain and establish.' Congress has used its power to create two inferior levels of federal courts. At the lowest level is the federal district court, the kind of court, for example, where Jane Roe began her case. The district courts are the basic trial courts of the federal judicial system and there are a total of ninety-four. Then above the district courts are the courts of appeals or 'circuit courts', of which there are twelve. Their task is to hear appeals from the district courts and federal regulatory commissions. Unlike the one-judge district courts, the courts of appeals are staffed by a large number of judges, currently ranging from six to twenty-six.

The federal courts, however, are only a part of the judicial picture in the United States. Each State has its own hierarchy of courts and there are also certain specialist courts, such as the Court of International Trade and the Court of Military Appeals (see Figure 3.1). Nevertheless, no matter which inferior court is concerned, the Supreme Court of the United States is the final court of appeals.

The Supreme Court's jurisdiction

Article III, Section 2, begins by stating that: 'The judicial Power shall extend to all Cases, in Law and Equity, arising under this Constitution, the Laws of the United States and Treaties made, or which shall be made, under their Authority ...'. This establishes the Supreme Court's jurisdiction over issues involving the Constitution, federal laws and treaties. An exception was made to this original grant of judicial power by the Eleventh Amendment to the Constitution, ratified in 1795. The Amendment withdrew the jurisdiction of the federal judiciary over cases between a State and a citizen of a different State or a foreign country. This was done to restore a common understanding of state immunity following the Supreme Court's decision in *Chisholm v. Georgia* (1793).[2]

The Court's jurisdiction is divided into two categories: original jurisdiction and appellate jurisdiction.

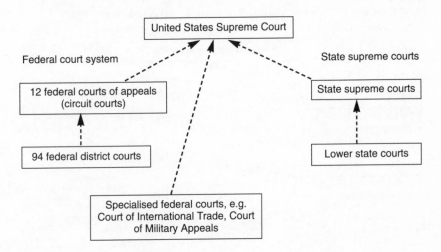

Figure 3.1 The American court system

Original jurisdiction

As we shall see below, the US Supreme Court is almost exclusively a court of appeals. There are a few areas, however, in which it has 'original jurisdiction', that is, in which it acts as the first court in which a case is heard. Article III of the Constitution (Section 2, paragraph 2) states: 'In all Cases affecting Ambassadors, other public Ministers and Consuls, and those in which a State shall be a Party, the supreme Court shall have original Jurisdiction.' In fact, the Supreme Court rarely takes up this invitation to act as a trier of facts and delegates such cases to other courts in the first instance. Thus while there may be over 7,000 cases on its docket, only a few are usually there under the Court's original jurisdiction.

Appellate jurisdiction

The real work of the Supreme Court stems from its appellate jurisdiction – the authority to hear and decide appeals from lower courts.
Article III, Section 2 states that apart from the cases assigned to its
original jurisidiction, 'the supreme Court shall have appellate Jurisdiction, both as to Law and Fact, with such Exceptions, and under such
Regulations as the Congress shall make'. Read in conjunction with the
first sentence of Article III quoted above, this means that the Court
can hear all appeals in cases arising under the Constitution, federal
laws and treaties. This includes cases which begin in state courts, if a
constitutional or federal statutory issue is involved (see Figure 3.2).

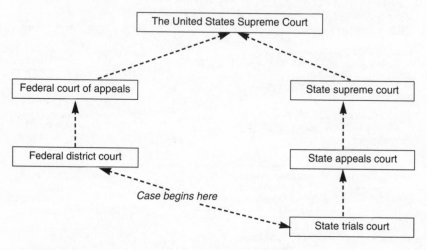

Figure 3.2 Paths of appeals to the United States Supreme Court

The sting in the tail, however, is that Congress is empowered to
make exceptions to this appellate jurisdiction. Although there is some
dispute as to what exactly is meant by this clause, it is usually read as
authorising Congress to strip the Court of its power to hear particular
categories of cases. Congress has frequently threatened to employ this
power when it has been displeased with the Court's decisions on particular subjects. In the contemporary period, for example, members of
Congress have attempted to take away the Court's appellate jurisdiction over such matters as abortion and school prayer. However, only
on one occasion to date has Congress succeeded in restricting the
appellate jurisdiction of the Court. That was in the immediate aftermath of the Civil War, when Congress removed the Court's authority

to hear certain kinds of appeals arising from the prosecution of civilians in military courts.

Categories of appellate jurisdiction

Appeals

Historically, there have been different kinds of appeal to the Supreme Court. Those known simply as 'appeals', for example, were notable because these were cases the Supreme Court was obliged to hear. However, throughout the twentieth century, Congress has gradually removed the mandatory elements of the Court's caseload in order to keep it within manageable limits. And this process culminated in the 1988 Judicial Improvements and Access to Justice Act, which eliminated virtually all mandatory appeals.

Writs of certiorari

The 1988 legislation means that virtually all cases argued before the Supreme Court today are there because the Justices have granted a writ of certiorari. This is a crucially important fact because grants of 'cert.' are discretionary: this in turn means that the Justices have virtually complete control of their agenda. This is just as well, since in the average year the Supreme Court will receive 5,000 or more petitions for a grant of certiorari. Out of these, the Court will usually select only between 90 and 150 for full review (Table 3.1). The rest are either summarily decided without full review or simply dismissed without explanation. Thus in the 1994–95 Supreme Court Term, the Justices accepted only 93 cases for full review out of a total of over 7,000 requests. And the current trend is for more appeals to be made, but fewer to be granted.

Granting certiorari

It is clear, then, that someone wishing to bring an appeal to the Supreme Court faces an uphill task in persuading the Justices to grant cert. or, as it is often said, to grant review. It is important therefore to understand the process by which thousands of petitions for review are whittled down to perhaps less than a hundred.

Table 3.1 The Supreme Court's docket, 1990–95

	1990*	1991*	1992*	1993*	1994*
Original jurisdiction	3	1	1	1	2
Appeals made	5,409	5,824	6,335	6,675	7,130
Appeals granted	141	120	97	99	93
Decided without review	109	74	109	64	66
Appeals denied	5,171	5,630	6,129	6,513	6,971**
% of appeals accepted for full review	2.6	2.1	1.5	1.5	1.3

*   A Supreme Court term runs from October to June/July of the following year.
** Totals do not always add up due to technicalities in the classification of cases.
Source: Adapted and simplified from Harvard Law Review, CIX, no. 1, p. 349.

When a petition for a grant of certiorari arrives at the Supreme Court, it is first scrutinised by the Justices' law clerks. These are assistants to the Justices. Each Justice is entitled to four clerks. These days, most of the Justices allow their clerks to work collectively within the 'cert. pool'. This avoids each Justice's clerks having to examine the same petitions and thus saves considerable time and effort. The petitions are simply shared out to different groups of clerks and their reports or 'memos', including a recommendation either to accept or deny review, are sent to the chambers of all the Justices who participate in the pool. There a second clerk will read the pool memo and annotate it or 'mark it up' for the Justice. Usually, the Justice will read only the pool memo and the mark-up.[3]

Discuss list and the 'rule of four'

The Chief Justice now prepares a list of cases he believes are worthy of discussion, although the other Justices can add any cases they wish to the list. Friday afternoons are set aside for discussion of the cases on the list. The critical factor which operates in this discussion is the 'rule of four'. If four of the nine Justices vote to grant review, then the case is taken: if not, it is dismissed or, occasionally, re-listed for later consideration when further information has been received.

Who really grants review?

It is worth pausing at this point to consider the role of the law clerks in the granting of review. Do their pool memos and mark-ups effectively decide whether review is granted or denied, especially if the Justices rarely read the actual petitions themselves at this stage?

According to the most detailed study, 'The clerks are not Richelieus or Rasputins, but that they play an important role in the cert. process simply cannot be denied.'[4] Law clerks are usually law school graduates of the highest calibre, who have spent a year working for a judge on a court of appeals before going on to spend a year at the Supreme Court. They clearly have important responsibilities in the cert. process, but most see their role as carrying out the wishes of their Justice. Thus, when they have learned their Justice's tendencies with regard to grants of review, their recommendations will follow suit. Moreover, the Justices themselves are confident that they can tell from the pool memo and their clerk's mark-up whether or not review should be granted.[5] It seems unlikely, then, that clerks are in a position to substitute their own views for those of the Justices.

Criteria for granting review

Given that the Justices usually select less than 200 cases for full hearing out of the thousands of petitions received, the question arises of what criteria they apply in making their selection.

Presumption against review

Perhaps the first thing to note is that there is effectively a presumption against granting review in any given case.[6] The sheer pressure on the Court's caseload usually means that if there are plausible grounds for denying review, then review will be denied. This, combined with the fact that many appeals are obviously frivolous, means that the great majority of cases are quickly dismissed.

Cases and controversies

Another basic point to be considered by the Justices is that Article III of the Constitution empowers them to decide only 'cases' and 'controversies'. There are a host of technical rules, often lumped together under the term 'justiciability', governing the definition of a case or controversy that the Justices may take. For example, the case must involve a genuine conflict between two parties, so the Court will not give an 'advisory opinion' in advance of a real legal dispute. Similarly, the Court is not supposed to entertain 'collusive suits', where the two parties have manufactured an artificial dispute to try to get a ruling from the Court.

Yet another facet is the 'ripeness' of a case. The Court may decide an issue or case is not ripe because it has not yet reached the point where the conflict is fully developed. Similarly, the Court may decide a case is 'moot' because the facts which originally supported it have changed or disappeared.

Allied to these technical qualifications is the notion of 'standing'. The party bringing the case only has the required standing to sue when he or she has suffered a real injury resulting from the action in dispute. This facilitates yet another aspect of justiciability, which is that a case is only taken when the Court can provide a suitable remedy for the alleged harm.

While all these aspects of justiciability appear to be technical and neutral, and designed to ensure that the legal issues are presented in their clearest light, the fact is that they are not always to be taken at face value. Justices are prone to retreat behind issues of justiciability when they want to avoid dealing with politically sensitive matters. On the other hand, the same Justices will dismiss arguments on grounds of justiciability if they are inconvenient.

In short, issues of justiciability can and are manipulated by the Justices for tactical reasons: and they almost never prevent the Court from getting to the substance of a case if it wishes to do so.

Inter-circuit conflict

With the remainder of the cases, certain key factors come into play. The Court usually feels bound to take a case which has raised a problem of inter-court or inter-circuit disagreement. This arises when a court of appeals has decided an issue in a way that conflicts with a decision on the same issue by another court of appeals or a state supreme court. Consistency is an essential feature in the law and the Supreme Court is obliged to resolve at least glaring inconsistencies in lower court decisions.

The federal government as petitioner

Another strong pointer to a successful petition for review is simply when the United States, through the Solicitor General, is the petitioner. The Solicitor General is successful in 80 per cent of his petitions for review, compared with about 3 per cent for all other lawyers.[7] This reflects not merely respect for the interests of the federal government, but also the fact that the Solicitor General carefully screens requests for review that come in from the myriad branches of the federal government.

Issue significance

Perhaps the most important criterion for granting review, however, is the most subjective and elusive of all. Quite simply a case will be heard because it raises an issue that the Justices deem substantial and important. Exactly what is a substantial question of constitutional or statutory law will vary from Justice to Justice and from one era to the next. As we saw in Chapter One, economic issues were deemed of prime importance in the age of industrialisation, but socio-moral issues are more central today. Nevertheless, because the Court's agenda is largely determined by the nation's political agenda, the Court often comes under enormous pressure to settle the major political conflicts of the day and, indeed, feels duty-bound to do so.

The politics of granting review

All the above factors may come into play in a particular case and may pull a Justice in different directions. What may in the end determine whether he or she votes to grant cert., however, is less the merits of the claim for review and more the likely vote if the case is accepted.

The formal process of granting review may appear relatively straightforward, but the Justices may already be engaged in strategic manoeuvres. Although there is little actual 'horse-trading' between Justices at the cert. stage, they may engage in what have been termed 'defensive denials' and 'agressive grants'.[8] A defensive denial occurs when a Justice believes that review should be granted on the merits of the case, but fears that a majority of her or his colleagues will reach a result of which he or she disapproves. He or she votes to deny review, therefore, in order to prevent the setting of a 'bad' precedent by the Court.

The aggressive grant presents the contrary scenario. The Justice does not think review should be granted on the merits, but votes to grant cert. anyway because the case presents a good opportunity for the Court to set a precedent with which he or she agrees.

In short, decisions about granting review are sometimes determined by the likely vote when the case itself is decided. An interesting example of this came to light recently when the late Justice Marshall's papers were released. The case was *Bowers v. Hardwick* (1986), which, as we saw in Chapter One, raised the issue of private homosexual acts. According to the Marshall papers, at first only Chief Justice Burger and Justice White wanted to take the case: they saw it as an opportunity to state that the Constitution does not protect the privacy of homosexual acts. Then the liberal Justices, led by Justice Brennan, moved for review in the belief that they had a majority for a ruling that the Constitution *did* protect such acts.

It emerged, however, that Justice Powell might not be with the liberals after all, so Brennan withdrew his support for cert. The conservative Justice Rehnquist then added *his* name in support of review, in the belief that the liberals would lose the vote. For their part, the other liberals did not withdraw their support for granting review along with Brennan, believing his pessimism to be unfounded. Brennan and the conservative Justices were right, however: the Court eventually voted 5 to 4 that the constitutional right to privacy did not extend to homosexual acts.[9]

Case procedures

Petitioners lucky enough to be granted review must pay a fee of $300, except for those too poor to afford it. They may file suit *in forma pauperis* (in the manner of a pauper). All cases granted review are given a docket number, showing the year of the Supreme Court Term and the order in which the case was filed. Thus the first case in the 1996 Term will receive the docket number 96–1. *In forma pauperis* cases are numbered slightly differently, beginning from 5001. Thus the second *in forma pauperis* case of the 1996 Term will be numbered 96–5002.

Despite the use of docket numbers, however, cases are always known by the names of the parties, with the petititoner's name coming first.

Oral argument

The clerk of the Court now requests written arguments or 'briefs' from the parties. The clerk will also schedule oral argument. Oral argument is the most dramatic public feature of a case. Each party's lawyer is allocated thirty minutes (or exceptionally an hour) to put her client's case to the nine Justices, while the public looks on. Oral argument can be a real ordeal for the lawyers. They may only be a few minutes into their presentation when a Justice interrupts with a question. Sometimes the lawyers are peppered with questions and comments throughout the entire thirty minutes and may not even get beyond the first major point they intended to make. However, although some of the Justices' questions may be intended to put the lawyer 'on the spot', others from a sympathetic Justice may be designed to be helpful.

For all the cut-and-thrust of oral argument, however, it is doubtful if cases are often won or lost because of it. For the Justices will already have studied the record of the case from the lower court and the written briefs submitted by counsel. The probability is that they will already have made up their minds before the oral argument takes place. Of course, an able lawyer may occasionally be able to clear up the doubts of one or more of the Justices, just as a poor oral argument may create doubts in the Justices' minds.

Briefs 'amicus curiae'

Between the grant of review and oral argument, another set of written documents may also be received at the Court. These are *amicus curiae* briefs, literally 'friend of the court' briefs. In fact, they are written arguments presented by interest groups who have a stake in the outcome of a case. The *amicus* briefs will contain facts, perspectives and arguments which hopefully will persuade the Justices to decide the case the way the group would like.

By no means all cases involve *amicus* participation, but most cases raising substantial issues of political significance are likely to attract interest groups. In the 1987 Term, for example, some 80 per cent of non-commerical cases before the Court involved *amicus* briefs.[10] Moreover, certain cases attract a huge number of *amici*: thus the 1989 *Webster* abortion case saw seventy-eight *amicus* briefs and the 1978 *Bakke* affirmative action case, fifty-eight. The Supreme Court usually welcomes the participation of *amici curiae*, particularly those which bring expert testimony to bear: an example would be the briefs filed in abortion cases by the American Medical Association.

It is very difficult to say, however, whether and to what extent the Justices are influenced by *amicus* briefs. Certainly the Justices make quite frequent explicit references in their written opinions to *amicus* briefs.[11] But this could simply be to buttress conclusions already reached by the Justices, rather than an indication of the persuasive power of the briefs. If nothing else, however, interest groups with a stake in Supreme Court litigation clearly think that it is important to file briefs to impress upon the Justices the social and political importance of the case concerned.

Case conference

Within a couple of days of hearing oral argument, the Justices will meet to discuss the case and take a preliminary vote. This case conference is conducted in complete secrecy, with only the Justices themselves present in the room. As a result of the strict secrecy, not everything is known about how the conference is conducted. However, the broad outlines are well-established.

The conference begins by each Justice shaking hands with all the others and then taking his or her allotted seat around a long, oblong table. The Chief Justice then introduces the first case, summarising the relevant facts, issues and law. In descending order of seniority the Justices then give their views. In the past it seems a vote was then taken in ascending order of seniority, the idea being that this way the newest Justices would not be pressured by the stated positions of the senior Justices. Today, however, it seems that this has been abandoned and that when the Justices first give their views they usually indicate their vote at the same time.

Surprisingly, perhaps, there is little attempt at conference to persuade other Justices of one's views. Rather, the main function of the conference is to determine which side of the argument has majority support.

Opinions

Once the conference has established the vote in a case, one of the Justices is assigned the task of writing the Court's Opinion – that is, the opinion of the majority if the Justices are not unanimous. The Court's Opinion is a formal attempt to explain the Court's decision and will usually summarise the facts of the case, state the relevant law and prior cases, and then provide a rationale for the conclusions reached.

Although Supreme Court Opinions are only read by a handful of people other than legal scholars and lawyers, they are nevertheless very important. Both the media and politicians will look to the scholars' analysis of an Opinion for guidance on whether a decision is sound or not. This is particularly true of controversial cases. It is in the interest of the Court, therefore, to make its Opinion as convincing as possible, since an unconvincing opinion will make the decision all the more vulnerable to attack.

The power to assign Opinions

The power to assign the Court's Opinion belongs to the Chief Justice, provided he is one of the majority. If he is in the minority camp, however, then the most senior (longest serving) Justice in the majority makes the assignment.

The Justice who has been assigned to write the Court's Opinion will eventually send drafts of his Opinion to the others. They will add comments, make suggestions and highlight any difficulties they have with the draft. Meanwhile, if the Court is split, the minority Justices will also be circulating their dissenting Opinions, criticising the Court's decision and reasoning.

Bargaining and compromise

It should be emphasised at this point that the vote in conference is only a preliminary vote. As draft Opinions, comments and dissents circulate around the Justices' chambers, the vote may change. Indeed, this is the stage of a case at which a good deal of bargaining and compromise between Justices may take place. Although a 5–4 vote is legally as authoritative a decision as a unanimous vote, realistically the more Justices who form the majority, the more commanding the decision. This is particularly true where a decision is likely to prove controversial and meet with resistance. The Justice writing for the Court, therefore, may well seek to persuade others to join his Opinion by accommodating their views on a particular point.

Perhaps the most famous instance of such accommodation occured in *Brown v. Board of Education* (1954). Chief Justice Earl Warren was convinced that if the Court was to declare racial segregation unconstitutional, it must do so unanimously. If not, the inevitable fierce denunciation of the decision in the South would latch on to dissenting votes and Opinions to argue that the Court had misinterpreted the Constitution. After much bargaining, Warren got his way – but at a price. Justice Reed, for example, only agreed to vote with the majority after a promise that the States would be allowed to implement desegregation gradually.

The assignment of Opinions may also be coloured by similar considerations. If, for example, the Chief Justice wishes to maximise the authority of a decision, he or she may well choose to assign it to him or herself as the Court's leader. This is what Warren did in *Brown*.

Or if her or his main concern is that an Opinion avoid radical statements, he or she may well assign the Opinion to a centrist Justice rather than one of the more extreme members of the majority. This is what Chief Justice Burger did in the landmark abortion case of *Roe v. Wade*. He hoped that by assigning the Court's Opinion to his moderate friend and fellow-Nixon appointee, Harry Blackmun, the new right to abortion would be narrowly framed in cautious terms, rather than in the grand statements of human rights that might have come from liberals such as William Douglas or William Brennan.

Unfortunately for Burger, it did not quite work out as planned. During the Opinion-drafting stage, Blackmun was pulled towards the liberals and Burger eventually felt obliged to write a concurring Opinion asserting that the Court's Opinion did not approve 'abortion on demand'. Burger became increasingly disenchanted with *Roe* and subsequent applications of its reasoning and in 1986 broke with it completely.

It often takes many months before the Court finally produces an Opinion which commands the support of a majority. Sometimes, indeed, there is no Opinion that commands a majority behind its reasoning, even if there are five votes to either uphold or overturn the lower court's decision. In these cases, there is a 'plurality Opinion', that is, the Opinion which commands more Justices' votes than any other: this is usually an Opinion supported by four or three Justices.

Multiple Opinions

Over recent decades, there has been a great proliferation in the number of concurring and dissenting Opinions and a concomitant decline in the number of unanimous decisions. As Table 3.2 indicates, well over half of the Court's decisions involve a dissent and barely one-third are fully unanimous. Along with this has come an increasing number of cases involving plurality Opinions. Such plurality Opinions are a problem because they mean that there is no majority reasoning behind a vote, and the decision is therefore lacking full authority as a precedent.

Table 3.2 Unanimity and dissent in court decisions, 1990–95

Term	Unanimous	With concurrence	With dissent
1990	35 (29%)	12 (10%)	73 (61%)
1991	25 (22%)	19 (17%)	70 (61%)
1992	35 (31%)	16 (14%)	63 (55%)
1993	25 (29%)	12 (14%)	50 (57%)
1994	28 (33%)	8 (9%)	50 (58%)

Source: Harvard Law Review, CIX, no. 1, 1995, p. 353.

The result of these developments is that the Court appears more fractured than ever before and, to some extent, its rulings seem less authoritative. For when even the majority Justices cannot agree on why they should vote together, there is a strong implication that the meaning of the Constitution is unclear and open to multiple interpretations, none of which is wholly convincing.

The causes of this fragmentation of the Court are not obvious, but certain factors seem to be part of the explanation. First, many of the issues decided by the Court in recent decades raise divisive moral, social and political questions that have not been litigated before. Moreover, these issues often have no direct touchstone in the text of the Constitution. These two factors combined mean that there are no clear guidelines for the Court to follow, making consensus more difficult to produce.

But whatever the causes of the Court's current fragmentation, multiple Opinions serve to remind us of the important fact that the Court is ultimately a body of nine autonomous individuals, who have no allegiances or ties other than their own conscience, philosophies and their understanding of constitutional and judicial obligations.

Announcing the decision

Once a decision is finally reached and all the Opinions written, the last step in the decision-making process is for the Court to announce the result to the public. Decisions are announced periodically throughout the term (October to June or July), although the major cases tend to be made public towards the end of the term.

The Justices appear in person at the Court and the Justice who has written the Court's Opinion makes the announcement. Occasionally, in a major case, the Justice may read aloud a large part of the Opinion, and the concurring and dissenting Justices may also state their positions. Usually, however, the Justice briefly summarises the case and the decision. Where controversial issues are involved, the decision now passes into the political realm to meet its fate.

Summary

The decision-making procedures of the Court are, for the most part, what one would expect from a court of law: calm, orderly and governed by routine and formal rules. It would be a grave error, however, to mistake process for substance. The Justices of the Supreme Court often possess fundamentally different views of the meaning of constitutional clauses and of their precise role in the American political system. These differences can lead to passionate disagreements over law, policy and, of course, politics. This will become apparent as we now turn to examine the concept and exercise of the power of judicial review.

Notes

1 A. Lewis, *Gideon's Trumpet*, 1964, New York, p. 5.
2 For a discussion of the complexities of the Eleventh Amendment, see Kermit L. Hall (ed.), *The Oxford Companion to the Supreme Court*, Oxford, 1992..
3 These details are taken from H. Perry, *Deciding to Decide: Agenda Setting in the United States Supreme Court*, Cambridge, Mass., 1991, Chapter 3.
4 *Ibid.*, p. 69.
5 *Ibid.*, pp. 70–1.
6 *Ibid.*, p. 218.
7 Hall (ed.), *The Oxford Companion*, p. 803.
8 Perry, *Deciding to Decide*, p.198.
9 As reported by Neil Lewis, *New York Times*, 25 May 1993.
10 L. Epstein, J. Segal, M. Spaeth and T. Walker, *The Supreme Court Compendium: Data, Decisions and Developments*, Washington, D.C., 1994, p. 581.
11 *Ibid.*, p. 582.

Four—Politics and judicial review

We saw in the previous chapter that the Supreme Court was created as a legal and judicial body, intended to complement rather than rival or duplicate the political branches of the federal government. Yet the very concept of judicial review in a constitutional democracy has proved to be inherently political. In this chapter, therefore, we examine the ways in which politics impinges upon judicial review and the various attempts which have been made to minimise or maximise the political potential of judicial review. We shall assess the extent to which the political characteristics of judicial review demand that we view the Court primarily as a political body.

Judicial interpretation: The traditional view

As we have seen (Chapter Two, page 48), in no. 78 of *The Federalist Papers*, Alexander Hamilton predicted that the Supreme Court would exercise not 'will', but 'merely judgement'. This means that the Justices would be free from political bias or influence in their decisions and simply undertake constitutional interpretation as a neutral exercise in logic and law. An analogy could be made with the categorisation of species: asked to say whether the whale was a fish or a mammal, marine biologists would note the fundamental characteristics of fish and mammals, then those of whales, and decide whether the whale fitted one category's set of criteria or the other. Our biologist would not be influenced by his or her preference for mammals over fish or society's views on whaling. Logic and established scientific knowledge and principles would be his or her guide.

Such a 'scientific' approach to law and constitutional adjudication held sway in legal circles well into the twentieth century. Take for example this statement by Justice Roberts in *US v. Butler*, in 1936. Roberts was writing for a 6–3 majority which declared unconstitutional the Agricultural Adjustment Act (AAA) of 1933. The AAA was the major effort under the New Deal to solve the terrible crisis in American agriculture, but the Court believed that Congress had exceeded its powers in levying a new processing tax to fund the programme. Justice Roberts denied, however, that the decision was influenced by political or policy considerations:

> When an act of Congress is appropriately challenged in the courts as not conforming to the constitutional mandate, the judicial branch has only one duty – to lay the article of the Constitution which is invoked beside the statute which is challenged and to decide whether the latter squares with the former. All the court does, or can do, is to announce its considered judgement upon the question. The only power it has, if such it may be called, is the power of judgement. This court neither approves nor condemns any legislative policy.

This view of constitutional interpretation as disembodied legal reasoning was dubbed 'mechanical jurisprudence' in order to emphasise how little the will of the judge mattered to the process.

Equally important to this traditional view was a method of legal reasoning which consisted of abstract principles and their logical extension and application. Although *applied* to different social, economic and political situations, these principles did not depend for their meaning upon the context of any particular case or issue. Justice George Sutherland exemplified this view in 1923 in *Adkins v. Children's Hospital*. This involved the constitutionality of a minimum wage law for women workers, who, it was argued, were more liable to be exploited by employers than men. Sutherland was quite unmoved by this socio-economic context, however, and stated that: 'In principle, there can be no difference between the case of selling labour and the case of selling apples.' He concluded that the law was simply a price-fixing statute and the fact that it involved labour, not apples, was not relevant to its constitutionality.

Whatever the merits of this traditional view of judging and constitutional interpretation, it served to maintain the belief that the Justices of the Supreme Court were politically objective in their work. Thus, when they pronounced a law unconstitutional, they spoke not for some political school or creed, but for the Constitution and those who framed it. They were legal mechanics who did not make law or policy, but rather 'discovered' law in the text of the Constitution and previous judicial decisions and then applied it to concrete cases.

Judicial interpretation: The modern view

Towards the end of the nineteenth century, the traditional view of legal reasoning came under attack as unrealistic both within and without the legal profession. One strand of this attack was called 'sociological jurisprudence'. This rejected the concept of law as abstract logic devoid of social context and argued instead that judges should understand and apply legal principles according to the relevant social realities. Thus, while there may be no difference in economic or legal principle between selling apples and selling one's labour, the nature and consequences of the two transactions could hardly be more different. The Supreme Court, therefore, might well strike down a law which fixed the price of apples but uphold another which guaranteed certain workers a minimum wage.

Indeed, sociological jurisprudence achieved a notable success as early as 1908 in the case of *Muller v. Oregon*. This involved a maximum hours statute for women factory workers that was similar in many respects to a law struck down by the Supreme Court in *Lochner v. New York*, decided three years before. Nevertheless, the lawyer for the workers, Louis D. Brandeis, amassed a great deal of evidence to show that the health of women was particularly vulnerable to long hours of work. The so-called 'Brandeis Brief' worked, as the Court voted unanimously to carve an exception from its usual principle that maximum hours laws were an unconstitutional infringement of freedom of contract.

An even broader attack on mechanical jurisprudence emerged at the beginning of the twentieth century in the form of 'legal realism'. The legal realists asserted that judges, including Justices of the Supreme Court, actually made law rather than discovered it. In other words, the meaning of any clause of the Constitution depended at least in part upon the predilections of the Justices – their political, economic and moral views and their concept of the public good. As Charles Evan Hughes, who was later to sit on the Court, put it in a famous aphorism: 'We are under a Constitution, but the Constitution is what the judges say it is.'

If the legal realists developed the understanding of the Justices of the Supreme Court as law-makers and policy-makers, then the 'judicial behaviouralists' of the 1960s pushed that concept to its limits. If the advocates of mechanical jurisprudence held that there was no *politics* in constitutional interpretation, then the behaviouralists asserted

that there was no *law* in constitutional interpretation. Most behaviouralists treated the legal cases that came before the Court as policy
questions pure and simple. And the Justices' decisions in those cases
were responses based on their policy preferences. Thus, as a leading
behaviouralist put it, 'The Justices themselves are goal orientated and
their basic goals are the same as those that motivate other political
actors.'¹ In short, Supreme Court Justices are, according to behaviouralists, little more than politicians disguised in judges' robes.

It can be seen that there have been conflicting views of the extent
to which politics is involved in the Supreme Court's major role as
interpreter of the Constitution. Which of these views is correct? Let
us now examine some of the main factors which can help us to come
to a conclusion.

Constitutional language

The first thing to note is that the meaning of the language in which
the Constitution is written is not always self-evident. To be sure, some
parts of the Constitution are crystal-clear: for example, Article II, Section 1 states unequivocally that no person shall be eligible for the office
of the presidency 'who shall not have attained the age of thirty-five
years, and been fourteen years a resident within the United States'.

Such clarity, however, is not typical of the Constitution. Take, for
example, the Eighth Amendment's ban on 'cruel and unusual punishments': reasonable people will certainly differ over what is a cruel punishment. For some, capital punishment is cruel, but for others not.
Some would say that certain methods of capital punishment, such as
hanging or the electric chair, are cruel, while other methods, like lethal
injection, are not. The point is clear: constitutional language is open,
even vague. It will bear different interpretations, yet the Justices must
decide which is the 'true' interpretation of the Constitution. Since the
Justices have a choice to make, the issue becomes how they make that
choice and with reference to what criteria. Above all, is it possible to
arrive at a definition of 'cruel' that is politically or morally neutral?

The examples of vague constitutional language could be multiplied
almost indefinitely; but it is worth noting at this point that much of
the contemporary agenda of the Court involves defining the meaning
of some of the most contentious concepts in political discourse. The
Fourteenth Amendment, for example, the source of many of the
Court's decisions on race and gender issues, demands an authoritative

interpretation of the phrase 'equal protection of the laws'. Any discussion of equality, it goes without saying, invites dispute, particularly
if the issue context is race or gender.

The First Amendment is another major focus of the Court's attention. Amongst other things, it states that 'Congress shall make no law
... abridging the freedom of speech, or of the press.' That may appear,
at first glance, to be clear since it forbids any such law to be passed.
Yet even a moment's reflection reveals a rich soil for contention: what
kinds of 'speech' and 'press' are protected? Is slander constitutional?
What about racial insults? Can the government prosecute someone for
mischievously shouting 'fire' in a cinema, just to enjoy the ensuing
panic? Or does the First Amendment protect hard-core pornographers
in publishing their magazines? Once again, then, constitutional interpretation requires the Justices to make choices and these choices are
full of political and moral meaning. They also have important implications for public policy.

At the very least, therefore, the Justices of the Supreme Court are
confronted with the temptation to use their power to decide legal controversies to further their own political and policy predilections. To
the extent that they yield, or are obliged to yield, to this temptation,
it can be suggested that the Supreme Court is a political body with a
major role in determining public policy.

Legal scholars and the Justices themselves have long been aware of
both the potential and the danger of allowing politics to overtake law
in the Court's work. There has, therefore, been considerable debate
about whether and how constitutional interpretation can be conducted
so as to minimise the elements of political choice. Several schools or
methods of interpretation have been the result.

Intentionalism

Those most opposed to 'political judging' argue that the Justices
should interpret the Constitution according to the intended meaning
of those who framed it. This doctrine of 'original intent' requires the
Court to ascertain, for example, what 'the equal protection of the laws'
meant to those in Congress who passed the Fourteenth Amendment
in 1868. Did they, for example, intend to outlaw racially segregated
schools or prevent restaurant owners from refusing to serve certain
racial groups?

Original intent is an attractive idea, because it means that the Justices follow not their personal values but those implanted in the Constitution. Constitutional values have explicitly been approved as the highest values of the nation, either because they were ratified in the original Constitution or because they have been sanctioned by the process of constitutional amendment. When the Court upholds the values of the framers, therefore, it acts merely as the mouthpiece of the nation's chosen supreme law.

There are, however, several problems with intentionalism which limit its usefulness. Two in particular merit attention here. The first is the problem of ascertaining the original intent of the framers. It is acknowledged by most constitutional historians that the framers did not always have a very clear idea of what they intended. This might be because they were only concerned with principles at the general level; or because, in addition, they actually disagreed among themselves over what their words were intended to mean. Much of the Constitution and most of its amendments involved a good measure of compromise among framers of different views. The wording of the Fourteenth Amendment, for example, emerged after a lengthy period of debate, proposal and counter-proposal and compromise. Eventually, the Thirty-Ninth Congress agreed simply 'to guarantee "equality", leaving it to others to determine what "equality" might entail'.[2] In short, it is very often difficult for the Justices to know what original intent requires in any particular case.

The second major problem with intentionalism is that it is by no means self-evident that Americans in the late twentieth century would wish to be governed by the ideas of those who lived in the late eighteenth century. When the Eighth Amendment was enacted in 1791, ear-clipping of prisoners was deemed neither cruel nor unusual. And the First Amendment's guarantee of free speech was only intended to prevent prior censorship of material and did not preclude prosecution for making derogatory statements about the government.

In order to overcome this objection, it is generally accepted that the modern Court must remain faithful to the general principle or value enshrined in the Constitution, but define it according to the moral and political vision of contemporary society. So, for example, it was agreed by the Supreme Court in *Trop v. Dulles* (1958) that the phrase 'cruel and unusual punishments' should be determined by 'the evolving standards of decency that mark the progress of a maturing society'.

This solves one problem, however, only at the cost of creating another. For it introduces a major element of choice for the Justices in that they are now required to define what is deemed cruel by contemporary society. But that society is itself divided over the issue of capital punishment. To which side of that division must the Justices adhere? And does not the duty to make that choice reintroduce the very temptation to consult one's own policy preferences that intentionalism was supposed to remove?

Textualism

The problems with intentionalism have led to various attempts to devise methods of interpretation which require the Justices to remain faithful to the text of the Constitution, while avoiding strict intentionalism's lack of clarity and historical rigidity. Thus, some advocate 'textualism' in which the 'plain meaning' of the words in the Constitution is controlling, thereby avoiding the need for a trawl through contradictory historical documents to discover the original intent of the framers.

Still others advocate 'moderate intentionalism' or 'moderate originalism' in which the Justices are expected to define some broad purpose behind a constitutional clause and then give it a contemporary gloss and application. Once again the school desegregation case of *Brown v. Board of Education* (1954) provides an illustration. While no historian produced persuasive evidence that the Fourteenth Amendment was intended or understood in 1868 to outlaw segregation, it is frequently argued that the Amendment's broad purpose did forbid it in 1954. That broad purpose was 'to secure all individuals a right to human dignity and equal standing before government, without regard to race or colour'.[3] Since few in the mid-twentieth century would deny that racial segregation placed a stigma on black Americans, then the constitutional standard of equal standing and dignity had clearly been breached.

Non-interpretivism

All these attempts to maintain the spirit of intentionalism, while still allowing the flexibility to adapt the Constitution to changing times and standards, increase the scope for judicial choice. And the greater the scope for judicial choice, the greater the chance that decisions will be made with reference to political and policy criteria – whether these stem from the Justices' personal views, public opinion, the government or some other source. In other words, the only realistic alternative to a strict intentionalism that yields results deemed unacceptable in modern society is a method of constitutional interpretation that allows the Supreme Court to make political choices.

Some have accepted this as inevitable and pushed it to its logical conclusion. They advocate a non-interpretive approach to constitutional adjudication, at least in those cases which involve civil rights and liberties. In essence, this means that the Court no longer needs to consult the Constitution, which is too limited a document to meet the civil liberties needs of a modern society.

Instead, the Justices must simply put forward the value or set of values which most advances their concept of a moral and just society and decide specific cases according to their tenets. Although granting the Court such sweeping political authority appears to violate democratic principles, non-interpretivists are convinced that the results are more likely to advance democracy than retard it. This, then, is a functional justification of judicial power, one that rests not on formal democratic theory, but rather on whether or not the Court does a good job of enhancing democratic values and social justice.

Judicial interpretation of statutes

Up to this point, we have concentrated upon issues arising from the Supreme Court's interpretation of the Constitution. It is very important to note, however, that the Court also plays a highly significant role in politics and government through its interpretation and application of laws passed by Congress. This is usually referred to as *statutory interpretation* or *statutory construction*.

Statutory interpretation raises many of the same questions as constitutional interpretation, although there is greater emphasis in statutory interpretation on discerning the original intent and meaning of the law. This is because statutes are usually more recent than constitutional clauses and, in theory, are more focused and explicit in their purpose and language.

Nevertheless, federal laws are frequently the product of bargaining and compromise within Congress, with the result that language is sometimes vague and intent by no means clear. And the less clear the original intent behind a statute, the more scope there is for judicial creativity and judicial policy-making.

In this respect, however, there is a major difference between statutory and constitutional interpretation. As we have already noted, the Court's interpretation of the Constitution can only be reversed by a constitutional amendment. Because this is so difficult to achieve, the Congress has no means of directly overturning a Supreme Court decision of which it disapproves. But Court decisions based on statutory interpetation is a very different matter. If the Justices construe the statutory language to yield a result that Congress dislikes, then Congress can simply amend the language of the statute to achieve the result it prefers.

For example, in 1990, in *Employment Division v. Smith*, the Court reviewed a case in which congressional general anti-drug legislation had the effect of banning certain Native American religious practices involving the use of peyote. In upholding the ban, the Court ruled that since the challenged drug law was general and not aimed at any particular religion, Congress need not prove that it had a 'compelling interest' in enacting a measure which had an incidental impact upon a certain religion.

This alarmed many members of Congress, including Senator Orrin Hatch of Utah. Utah is the home of the Mormon religion in the United States and Hatch was concerned that the *Smith* decision might someday work against Mormons or other religious minorities. He got together with Senator Edward Kennedy, a staunch supporter of civil liberties in general, and they co-sponsored the Religious Freedom Restoration Act of 1993. This squarely reversed *Smith* and thus required government to demonstrate some 'compelling' reason before it could interfere even incidentally with religious practices.

Paradoxically, the relative ease with which Congress can reverse Supreme Court decisions based on statutory construction may encourage the Justices to be creative. To put it simply, the Court knows that if it 'gets it wrong', then the Congress can take appropriate action. If, on the other hand, Congress is pleased with the Court's innovation, then judicial policy-making proves acceptable as a substitute for legislation. That may not square with the formal requirements of democratic procedure, but it is a time-saving and pragmatic alternative. In effect, the Court thereby acts as an agent of the legislature, with the legislature retaining the power to correct judicial mistakes.

The Court has made some notable policy innovations through statutory interpretation, with the outstanding example being its creative application of the Civil Rights Act of 1964. In 1979, in *United Steelworkers v. Weber*, a 7–2 majority of the Justices upheld a minority-race preference scheme operated by the Kaiser Aluminum company. The scheme involved giving places on a skills training programme to blacks and whites in equal numbers, regardless of other factors such as seniority. A white employee, Brian Weber, failed to gain a place on the scheme, even though he had more seniority than some of the African-Americans who had been given a place. Weber alleged that this clearly violated part of the 1964 Act forbidding preferential treatment on grounds of race. Not only did the language of the Act seem clearly to support Weber's case, but the history of its passage made expressly clear that Congress did not intend to permit the kind of scheme operated by Kaiser Aluminum.

**The 1964 Civil Rights Act
Section 703(d)**

It shall be unlawful employment practice for any employer, labour organization or joint labour-management committee controlling apprenticeship or other training or retraining, including on-the-job training programmes, to discriminate against any individual because of his race, colour, sex, or national origin in admission to, or employment in, any programme established to provide apprenticeship or other training.

The Court, however, said that its decision was based not a literal interpretation of the Act, but on its broader purpose of opening up to African-Americans jobs from which they had previously been excluded. And one of the majority Justices, Harry Blackmun, said that if Congress did not approve of the Court's interpretation, then it could amend the Act to make that clear.

Congress did not rebuke the Court and thus gave tacit approval to this judicial amendment to federal legislation. In other words, on this occasion, most members of Congress approved a liberal, non-interpretivist approach to statutory construction and a major piece of judicial policy-making.

Judicial role philosophy

The twentieth century has thus seen an increasingly insistent assault upon the idea of politically objective judges in constitutional and statutory interpretation. While intentionalists still argue for the possibility of at least a significant measure of neutrality in constitutional interpretation, and the desirability of such an approach, many others are now convinced neither of the possibility nor of the desirability.

But is all this any more than an academic debate between scholars and judges? Most certainly, yes. For it goes to the very heart of the nature of the Supreme Court and its role in American government. Perhaps the most important distinction between the political and judicial functions is that the former involves the selection of values and policies, while the latter involves merely the explication and application of these values. In other words, what makes a judge a judge (and not a politician) is that he or she does not choose what values, policies or laws govern society.

Of course, that clear distinction in the abstract collapses in reality. Politics and law are, and always have been, intertwined. Nevertheless, if we take the two extremes as opposite ends of a continuum, we can place the Court, or an individual Justice, towards one end of the continuum or the other. And the nearer it gets to the political end, the more the Court loses its legitimacy as a judicial body. At the extreme, it becomes not a court of law, but a super-legislature with the power to override the Congress and President on at least some important matters of public policy.

Judicial activism and restraint

These debates over the possibility and desirability of keeping politics out of constitutional interpretation have led to the development of associated schools of 'judicial role philosophy'. Such role philosophies go beyond issues of interpretive method, however, and also encompass a view of the relationship between the Court and the rest of the governmental system. In particular, it focuses on the proper relationship between the Court and the two other branches of the federal government, the Congress and the presidency.

We can identify two main judicial role philosophies, those of 'judicial self-restraint' and 'judicial activism'. Once again, however, we should remember that Justices rarely fall neatly into one category or the other.

The case for judicial self-restraint

Those Justices and legal scholars who advocate judicial self-restraint do so for a number of fundamental reasons. First, they are particularly conscious of the tension between judicial review and democracy. In order to avoid as far as possible a situation in which unelected judges appear to usurp the policy-making functions of legislatures, advocates of self-restraint counsel the Court to be cautious in the exercise of judicial review. In effect, they believe that the less intrusive the Court, the more democracy can operate.

Second, restraintists have grave doubts about the capacity or ability of the Court to make sound public policy. After all, the Justices may have no great knowledge of, say, economic policy or welfare policy. And unlike the Congress and the President, they do not have vast numbers of advisers with the appropriate levels of knowledge and expertise. Once again, then, the Court should be cautious in striking down the considered policy judgments of the elected branches of government, because it may in its ignorance do more harm than good. Justice Oliver Wendell Holmes expressed this aspect of judicial restraint, when he dissented from the Court's decision striking down the minimum-wage law in Adkins v. Children's Hospital (1923):

> When so many intelligent persons, who have studied the matter more than any of us, have thought that the means are effective and are worth the price, it seems to me impossible to deny that the belief reasonably may be held by reasonable men.

The third major concern of restraintists is that there are few means of rectifying bad decisions by the Court. Because the Court's decisions can only be overturned by the rarely-used instruments of constitutional amendment or the withdrawal of appellate jurisdiction (see Chapter Three), there are few formal checks on the Court's power. The Justices should exercise caution, therefore, because, as Justice Harlan Stone advised his colleagues in US v. Butler (1936):

> while unconstitutional exercise of power by the executive and legislative branches of the Government is subject to judicial restraint, the only check on our own exercise of power is our own sense of self-restraint.

Justice Robert Jackson had a similar thought in mind when he reminded his fellow Justices in Brown v. Allen (1953) that 'We are not final because we are infallible, but we are infallible only because we are final.'

It can be seen that the main thrust of judicial self-restraint is that the Court should only use the power of judicial review sparingly. Above all, it should only pronounce a law, especially a federal law, unconstitutional when there is a clear violation of a specific constitutional clause.

The Ashwander Rules of self-restraint

In order to stay within the boundaries counselled by judicial self-restraint, Justices have devised certain guidelines and practices. One of the first attempts to codify these practices was undertaken by Justice Louis Brandeis in his opinion in *Ashwander v. TVA* (1936). The two main elements of these so-called 'Ashwander Rules' were, first, that whenever possible, the Court would avoid making constitutional decisions at all. Thus, the Court would not anticipate a question of constitutional law; it would not dispose of a case on constitutional grounds, if the issue could be settled under statute law; and, where a constitutional ruling was inevitable, it would be no broader than that required by the facts of the particular case before it.

The second main element is the most important of all: that if there existed any reasonable construction of the statute under challenge that would render it constitutional, then the Court should adopt that construction. In other words, if a law can be understood in two different ways – one constitutional, the other not – then the Court should accept the former understanding.

There are other canons of judicial self-restraint which are also of considerable importance. Closely associated with the Ashwander Rules is the notion of 'presumptive constitutionality': this means simply that every law under challenge before the Court is presumed constitutional unless clearly shown to be otherwise. All the benefit of the doubt goes to the law rather than the challenge.

Political questions

Then again the Court has devised for itself the concept of a 'political question' that the judiciary should avoid. A 'political question' is one to which the Court either cannot provide a remedy, and is therefore 'non-justiciable', or one which the Constitution is deemed to have left wholly to the other branches of government for resolution. There is, however, much scepticism among scholars about the 'political question'. It is ill-defined and subject to varying interpretations, creating the impression that it is actually a device for allowing the Court to dodge issues which are politically sensitive. In recent decades the Supreme Court and lower federal courts have employed the 'political questions' doctrine in refusing to deal with cases challenging the legitimacy of presidential war-making powers. Such cases emerged involving the Vietnam War, the Reagan administration's deployment of military personnel in El Salvador and President Bush's use of the armed forces during the Gulf War, for example. The Supreme Court and lower courts essentially took the line that issues of war-making were matters which the Constitution left for the legislative and executive branches to decide between themselves.[4] However, the Constitution makes no exceptions to the Court's authority, either for war-making, or indeed, any other area of policy. Nevertheless, the Court feels the need to avoid becoming involved in certain highly-charged political and constitutional wrangles and the 'political questions' doctrine is one means of doing so.

At the heart of self-restraint, then, is the notion of judicial deference to the elected branches of government. A self-restrained Supreme Court will seek to minimise clashes with the Congress, the President and the state legislatures and will therefore try to avoid resolving cases on the basis of constitutional rulings. It is a reluctant player in the policy-making process because it believes that a republican form of government is one in which the people and their chosen representatives should exercise legislative power. Only when the Constitution speaks clearly and a law unmistakably violates that pronouncement will the Court wield its mighty power to declare a law unconstitutional.

If one thought above all others is constantly in the mind of a Justice who advocates self-restraint, it is that personal views of good public policy should never be allowed to influence her or his interpretation of the Constitution. As Justice Felix Frankfurter, amongst the greatest of such advocates, wrote in *Board of Education v. Barnette* (1943):

> As a member of this Court I am not justified in writing my private notions of policy into the Constitution, no matter how deeply I may cherish them, or how mischievous I may deem their disregard.

The self-restrained Justice, therefore, seeks to eliminate her or his personal policy views by deferring to the legislature, deferring to some form of original intent, or by deferring to the decisions of prior courts by following precedent. If a majority of the Justices practise self-restraint, then the Supreme Court will only rarely make a dramatic entry into the politics and government of the United States.

The case for judicial activism

Judicial activists believe that the kinds of deference noted above are unwarranted. They are confident about the legitimacy of judicial review in a constitutional democracy and see no need to exhibit especial deference to the elected branches of government. Thus, when the Court invoked such restraintist arguments to support its decison allowing legislatures unprecedented powers to regulate wages in *West Coast Hotel v. Parrish* (1937), the conservative activist Justice George Sutherland emphasised in his dissent that:

> The people by their Constitution created three, separate, distinct, independent and co-equal departments of government. The government structure rests, and was intended to rest, not upon one or any two, but upon all three of these fundamental pillars.

Neither are activists particularly concerned by the complexity or sensitivity of cases. In the legislative reapportionment case of *Baker v. Carr* (1962), for example, when the 'political question' doctrine was raised, along with arguments about judicial capacity, the liberal activist Justice William Douglas was unperturbed:

> It is said that any decision in cases of this kind is beyond the competence of the Courts. Some make the same point as regards the problem of equal protection in cases involving racial segregation. Yet the legality of claims and conduct is a traditional subject for judicial determination.

Still another line of division between activists and restraintists is their attitude towards precedent. As noted above, adherence to precedent, though not absolutely binding, is very important to advocates of self-restraint. They see it a crucial factor in making judicial decision-making a legal process, since it helps to ensure stability and continuity in the law and to minimise the scope for judicial innovation. Activists admit respect for precedent is important, but not so important as to prevent them from overruling a prior decision that they think was simply wrong. A fascinating exchange on this subject took place in the major abortion rights case of *Planned Parenthood v. Casey* (1992). Justices O'Connor, Kennedy and Souter intimated that they believed the Court had erred in creating a new right to abortion in *Roe v. Wade* (1973). Nevertheless, they voted to uphold *Roe*'s central ruling out of respect for precedent. In their joint opinion, they argued that the Court must follow *Roe* because many women had come to rely upon it in organising their lives and they were entitled to count upon its continuation in force. They also believed that precedent should be upheld in order to demonstrate that the Supreme Court was indeed a court of law that did not change its mind quickly under political pressure of the kind exerted by the pro-life movement.

Planned Parenthood v. Casey (1992): Opinion of Justices O'Connor, Kennedy and Souter

The Opinion recognised that a constitutional decision by the Court on such a divisive issue as abortion would inevitably lead to attempts to force the Court to reverse itself in later cases. But the Court must hold firm to its decision in the face of such pressure, for:

> only the most convincing justification under accepted standards of precedent could suffice to demonstrate that a later decision overruling the first was anything but a surrender to political pressure, and an unjustified repudiation of the principle on which the Court staked its authority in the first place. So to overrule under fire in the absence of the most compelling reason would subvert the Court's legitimacy beyond any serious question ...
>
> It is true that diminished legitimacy may be restored, but only slowly. Unlike the political branches, a Court thus weakened could not seek to regain its position with a new mandate from the voters, and even if the Court could somehow go to the polls, the loss of its principled charac-ter could not be retrieved by the casting of so many votes. Like the char-acter of an individual, the legitimacy of the Court must be earned over time.'

Justice Scalia, on the other hand, was scathing about this view of the importance of precedence. For him, a wrong decision should be reversed whatever the context or consequences. Justice Scalia's posi-tion raises a problem within the concept of judicial activism. Scalia himself would argue that overturning a wrong precedent is not activism, especially if the precedent itself was the product of judicial activism. In restoring what he believes to be the true and original con-stitutional interpretation, Scalia could claim to be pursuing restraint.

However, willingness to overturn precedent should be classified as a characteristic of activism, simply because, whatever the motive behind the reversal, it serves to free the Justice to impose his or her own reading on the Constitution. As with other aspects of judicial activism, it is this relative lack of deference to other 'authorities' which is distinctive.

It can be seen that judicial activism and self-restraint are not tied to particular political creeds. An activist may be conservative, like

Sutherland, or liberal, like Douglas. It is true that conservative Justices invariably deny that they are activists, insisting that they are merely upholding the original meaning of the Constitution. This is not always convincing, however. Thus the conservative majority on the Court in the early twentieth century read their own views of political economy into the Constitution, as when they insisted that 'liberty' in the Fourteenth Amendment meant a 'liberty of contract' that disbarred most forms of regulation. They also did not hesitate to enforce liberty of contract against state and federal authorities, no matter how great the need felt by these policy-makers. In fact, in many respects, they exhibited the same characteristics as the liberal activists of the Warren Court in the 1950s and 1960s.

Ultimately, whatever the professed motives behind it, judicial activism has the result of thrusting the Supreme Court to the centre stage of American politics. In contrast to a restraintist Court, an activist Court will be regularly involved in politics, not simply because it resolves constitutional controversies, but because it resolves them according to its own confident view of what the Constitution demands.

The Political Context of Judicial Review

So far in this chapter, we have examined the ways in which politics infiltrates the Court's work through the interpretive and role philosophies of the Justices themselves. Is is also important to acknowledge, however, that forces exterior to the Court play a part in creating the political dimensions of judicial review.

The most important aspect of this is that other political bodies recognise that decisions of the Supreme Court, however arrived at, may have important political consequences. Quite irrespective of whether the Court applies mechanical jurisprudence or non-interpretivism, its decision contributes to or even determines public policy on that matter. Whether it likes it or not, then, the Court is a policymaker of importance in the American political system.

As a result, other political bodies treat the Court as a policy-making institution and try to influence its decisions. We will see in Chapter Five that the President and the Senate try to manipulate the process of appointing Justices, so as to entrench their own political views on the Court. But beyond this, they also try to influence the Court's deliberations and decisions on a case-by-case basis. So do interest groups.

Influence

The President and the Court

Apart from his appointive powers, the President is able to exert political influence on the Court through the Department of Justice. At the head of the Department is the Attorney General, appointed by the President subject to Senate confirmation. The Attorney General may decide to set out a presidential agenda with regard to the Supreme Court, as did Edwin Meese during President Reagan's second term. Meese launched a public campaign which argued, amongst other things, that the Court had become too activist and should return to the days when the doctrine of original intent dominated constitutional interpretation. While such a campaign may not directly influence what the Justices do, it does represent a conscious effort to re-shape the political context of the Court's work. In that sense, it is an attempt to bring pressure to bear on the Court.

The Solicitor General

The President can wield more direct influence, however, through the office of the Solicitor General, the member of the Justice Department with specific responsibilities for the Supreme Court. The Solicitor General's principal task is to represent the government of the United States before the Supreme Court. This he or she may do in a number of ways which afford the administration considerable influence. First, where the government has a stake in the issue, the Solicitor General brings appeals before the Court. Second, the Solicitor General may intervene in a case as *amicus curiae* and may even argue part or the whole of a case before the Court. Third, the Court may take the initiative itself and invite the Solicitor General to submit a brief setting out the government's views on an issue.

That the Court invites the Solicitor General's opinion indicates the high esteem in which the Justices hold the office. Indeed, the Solicitor General is sometimes dubbed 'the Tenth Justice', because of the high value of her or his work. It also suggests the influence which he or she can wield. This is further supported by the fact that, as we saw in the previous chapter, any request for appeal by the Solicitor General will at least be discussed by the Justices and about 80 per cent of those requests will actually be granted.[5]

The Solicitor General is thus in a position to influence both the agenda of the Court and its actual decisions. This influence, however, is dependent upon the Solicitor General being viewed by the Court as above mere partisan politics. If the Solicitor General behaves too much like any other politically-motivated lawyer, then her or his influence will dwindle and he or she will be treated just like any other lawyer.

This was the fate that befell Charles Fried, a Solicitor General in the Reagan administration. Fried was under pressure from Meese and other conservatives in the Justice Department to continue to press the administration's views on social issues, including abortion and affirmative action, even when the Court had repeatedly rejected them. It is widely believed that such partisan persistence by Fried led to his role becoming counter-productive – his mere appearance, for example, was supposedly enough to lose the government the vote of Justice Stevens.

Nevertheless, provided the Solicitor General avoids blatant partisanship, her or his views about what the Court should decide will at least be carefully considered by the Justices. And apart from the appointment process, he or she may be the President's best means of influencing Supreme Court decisions.

Congress

Until 1978, the Congress relied upon the Solicitor General to defend its legislation in the Courts. Growing concern about the perceived politicisation of that office, however, led the Senate to create the Office of the Senate Legal Counsel (SLC). The SLC is a non-partisan lawyer who represents the Congress in much the same way as the Solicitor General represents the United States government. Nonetheless, the office has not achieved anything like the same status with the Court as has the Solicitor General. Its mere existence, however, indicates a further blurring of the line between law and politics.

The most obvious way in which the Congress invites judicial intervention in policy-making is by deliberately framing legislation in unclear or incomplete terms. Congress may choose to do this either because agreement between legislators on particular points cannot be achieved or because unclear language may help to avoid provoking a presidential veto. This 'supplementary law-making' may lead to considerable judicial policy innovation, as happened with the Court's use of the 1964 Civil Rights Act to promote affirmative action. Congress failed to define in the Act either what was meant by the term 'discrimination' or what remedial measures would be required or permitted. The Court, as well as the federal bureaucracy, were thus left to fill in these most important aspects of the legislation.

However, just as Congress is sometimes content to give the Court great latitude in fleshing out its legislation, it is also concerned on other occasions to try to influence the Court's decisions. This is particularly the case, of course, when an act of Congress is challenged as unconstitutional.

It should be said immediately that the Court is far more wary of striking down federal acts, as opposed to state legislation. Thus even the highly activist Warren Court struck down only 23 federal statutes in whole or in part, compared with 189 state laws.[6] Congress can be sure, therefore, that the Court will not overturn its legislation lightly.

Nevertheless, Congress will sometimes feel the need to present its views directly to the Court and this it can do by filing an *amicus curiae* brief. Indeed, members of Congress are taking this route with increasing frequency these days. Thus whereas in the 1970s there were just seven cases in which members of Congress filed an amicus brief, the 1980s witnessed fifty-seven such interventions.[7]

A notable example of this occured in *Harris v. McRae* (1980), where the Court had to consider the constitutionality of a congressional ban on using federal Medicaid funds to pay for the abortions of poor women. Congress feared that if the Court overturned the ban, it would effectively be usurping the traditional 'power of the purse' enjoyed by Congress. Consequently, 238 members of Congress, led by the Speaker of the House of Representatives Jim Wright, filed an *amicus* brief sternly warning the Justices 'to respect the foundations of our government of separate and limited powers, of which the power of the purse is democratically entrusted to the Congress'.[8]

In short, depending on the issue, Congress will either invite the Court to play an expansive role in politics and policy-making or strongly urge the Court to stick to its areas of competence. Either way, however, the Court has political as well as legal factors to take into consideration.

Interest groups

Interest groups provide a vital link between the Court and the nation's politics. While they do not directly lobby judges in the way they do legislators, there are mechanisms which allow them to bring their members' views to the attention of the Court.

Interest groups as *amici curiae*

The oldest and still most widely used of these is the *amicus curiae* brief. Literally meaning *friend of the court*, the brief was originally designed to permit those with special expertise of value to the Court to present arguments, even though they were not actual parties to the case. Over the years, however, it has become a vehicle for all kinds of interest groups to throw their weight behind one party or the other. And whereas once it was comparatively rare either for one group to become involved in a large number of cases or for many groups to be *amici curiae* in a single case, interest group participation through the *amicus* brief is now very common. In the 1987 Supreme Court Term, for example, 80 per cent of non-commerical cases involved *amicus* briefs. And in major cases hundreds of groups may participate, though many band together to file just one 'coalition brief'. Nevertheless, in the 1989 abortion case of *Webster v. Reproductive Health Services*, for example, seventy-eight actual *amicus* briefs were filed – forty-seven by pro-life groups and thirty-one by pro-choice groups.[9]

Despite all this *amicus* activity, however, it is far from clear how much influence these briefs have over the Court's decision. Some groups may have more influence than others. For example, respected professional organisations, such as the American Medical Association, may have most influence because they can offer the Justices expert medical knowledge. Ideological groups, however, such as the National Organization for Women or Concerned Women for America, may find their views discounted as too partisan.

The fact that the Justices do quite frequently make reference to arguments and material contained in *amicus* briefs in their Opinions may suggest significant influence. On the other hand, such references may merely be used bolster a position the Justice had arrived at anyway. Nevertheless, the *amicus* brief is certainly a means by which policy and political arguments are brought before the Court. And at least occasionally, a brief may make a difference to the Court's decision.

Interest groups as case sponsors

Some interest groups, however, play a much more important role in the exercise of judicial review – they actually bring cases to the Court. Such groups are usually dedicated to an ideological position or a policy objective and have the resources to sustain a long litigation campaign. For the most part, they are also liberal groups who are seeking to use judicial review as a means of introducing social reform.

One of the first of these groups was the American Civil Liberties Union (ACLU). Although non-partisan in the sense that it defends the liberties of those on both the left and the right of American politics, its dedication to the cause of individual rights tends to find it siding with progressive causes.

Founded in 1920, the ACLU first achieved fame in 1926 in the so-called 'Monkey Trial', when it sponsored John Scopes' fight to teach the theory of evolution in a Tennessee school, despite a state law forbidding it. Since then it is estimated that ACLU lawyers have participated in 80 per cent of the major cases involving civil liberties that have been decided by the Court.[10] Thus, for example, the ACLU created its Women's Rights Project in the 1970s which led directly to a series of victories in gender equality cases.

But the explosion of interest group litigation really occurred in the wake of the campaign by the National Association for the Advancement of Colored People (NAACP) to end racial segregation in law. With the NAACP's victory in *Brown v. Board of Education* (1954), it became apparent that the Supreme Court offered certain disadvantaged groups a better chance of success than the traditional political arena. The Justices were often more enlightened in their views on minority rights than legislators. More important still, their appointment for life freed them from the need to pander to the prejudices of the electoral majority. Finally, winning in the Supreme Court offered the prospect of total victory, in that a constitutionalised right was applicable in all States and stood very little chance of being reversed in the future. To the extent that their resources allowed them, then, other groups followed the NAACP's example.

An offshoot of the NAACP, its Legal Defence and Educational Fund, Inc. (LDF), played the leading role in the campaign to end capital punishment. It actually succeeded in stopping all executions between 1968 and 1977 and persuaded the Court in *Furman v. Georgia* (1972) to declare all existing death penalty statutes unconstitutional. As noted above, the Women's Rights Project of the ACLU managed the litigation campaign for greater gender equality under the law in the 1970s. And lawyers from the National Organization for Women led the campaign to secure abortion rights.

Thus interest groups have done a great deal to set the modern agenda of the Supreme Court. They have been important in persuading the Court to confront issues it may not otherwise have taken. Moreover, they have often succeeded in persuading the Court to throw caution to the wind and read new, significant rights into the Constitution. By carefully selecting which cases to bring before the Justices and by preparing expert legal and constitutional arguments, interest groups have helped to engender the modern role of the Supreme Court in American government. Indeed, without the resources and energies of interest groups, it is now difficult to imagine how the Supreme Court could operate effectively.

Public opinion

In analysing government institutions in liberal democracies, it is always necessary to ask whether they are responsive to public opinion. On the other hand, as we have seen throughout this book, the Supreme Court was intended to be free of direct popular pressures. The whole purpose of the Supreme Court is to be able to resist public opinion when it conflicts with the commands of the Constitution.

In the case of the Supreme Court, therefore, responsiveness to public opinion may be a cause for criticism rather than praise. Nevertheless, the Court has to live in the real world and that world is a highly political one. Over the long term, the Court cannot simply ignore public opinion, since that will diminish both the respect in which it is held and, therefore, its power.

Once again, then, the Supreme Court is forced to tread a fine line. If it listens too closely to public opinion, it fails to carry out its prime duty of upholding constitutional values. If it ignores strongly held public opinion, however, it risks losing its authority.

Fortunately for the Justices, there are factors which help them to solve this dilemma. And the first is that the great mass of the public are generally ignorant of what the Court actually does. Thus in a 1990 survey, less than a quarter of Americans knew how many Justices there are and only about one-third could name any of the Justices.[11]

Public knowledge of the Court's decisions is also low: about three-fifths of Americans cannot describe any Court ruling they like or dislike or accurately describe even the Court's great landmark decisions.[12] Such ignorance is hardly likely to persuade members of an institution charged with defying popular pressure in the name of the Constitution to kowtow to public opinion.

Ignorance does not necessarily absolve the Court from public criticism, of course. Like all governmental bodies in the contemporary United States, the Court does not benefit from a great deal of public confidence. Nevertheless, it consistently does better than either Congress or the presidency in this respect. In 1986, for example, 30 per cent of those surveyed expressed a great deal of confidence in the Court, compared with 21 per cent for the presidency and 16 per cent for Congress.

There would seem to be, therefore, a combination of public ignorance and public respect which helps the Court to ignore direct public pressure. This does not mean, however, that the Court's decisions and public opinion consistently and widely diverge. There are issues on which the Court and the public are at loggerheads: decisions banning school prayer or ending capital punishment, for example. That said, the Court's decisions are generally in tune with public opinion – and to about the same extent as legislative policies. As the most detailed study of the Court and public opinion put it:

> Overall, the evidence suggests that the modern Court has been an essentially majoritarian institution. Where clear poll margins exist, three-fifths to two-thirds of Court rulings reflect the polls. Precise comparisons with other policy makers can be offered only tentatively. However, the modern Court appears to reflect mass public opinion as often as do popularly elected office holders.[13]

In spite of this, there is little or no direct relationship between the Court and the people. The Court does not usually influence public opinion through its decisions and the public does not usually directly influence the Justices.

The crucial link between public opinion and Supreme Court decisions, then, is the views, policies and likely reactions of the national legislators who the public elects. Federal laws do usually reflect public opinion and the Supreme Court is generally deferential to those laws. In other words, by generally deferring to congressional policies, the Court finds itself in tune with public opinion.

Public opinion is thus mediated by Congress and can only rarely be considered a direct influence upon the Court's decisions. Nevertheless, because a generally ignorant and apathetic public may become aroused by particular decisions, and demand that Congress do something about them, the Court may bear in mind such likely reactions when adjudicating controversial cases. In that sense, public opinion is an important but indirect and sporadic political influence on the Court.

Summary

In this chapter we have seen that a combination of factors bring politics into the exercise of judicial review. From the outside, politicians and interest groups seek to set the Court's agenda and then influence its decisions. Although they may couch their arguments in legal and constitutional terms, their motivations are profoundly political. Meanwhile, even Justices trying earnestly to think and act as judges rather than politicians find that constitutional interpretation permits or requires them to import political considerations into their deliberations. Together, then, these factors mean that the Supreme Court is a political body, even if its legal and judicial aspects ensure that it is not *simply* a political body.

The exercise of judicial review calls for good political as well as judicial skills. Thus the effective fulfilment of the Court's role depends in no small measure on the qualities of those who are chosen to serve as its Justices. In the next chapter, therefore, we examine who gets appointed to the Supreme Court and how and why?

Notes

1 G. Schubert, *Judicial Policy-Making*, Glenview, Ill., 1965, p. 164, fn. 9.
2 A. Kull, *The Color-Blind Constitution*, Cambridge, Mass., 1992, p. 87.
3 A. Cox, *The Court and the Constitution*, Boston, 1987, p. 260.
4 J. Grossman, 'Political Questions', in K. Hall (ed.), *The Oxford Companion to the Supreme Court of the United States*, New York, 1992, pp. 651–3.
5 H. Perry, *Deciding to Decide: Agenda Setting in the United States Supreme Court*, Cambridge, Mass.,1991, pp. 93 and 128.
6 L. Epstein J. Segal, M. Spaeth and T. Walker, *The Supreme Court Compendium: Data, Decisions and Developments*, Washington, D.C., 1994, adapted from Tables 2–12 and 2–13, pp. 96–128.
7 *Ibid.*, Table 7–2, pp. 551–2.
8 Brief of Rep. Jim Wright *et al.* as *Amici Curiae, Transcripts of Records and Briefs 1979*, CCXX, p. 15.
9 K. Kolbert *et al.*, 'The *Webster Amicus Curiae* Briefs: Perspectives on the Abortion Controversy and the Role of the Supreme Court', *American Journal of Law and Medicine*, XV, 1989, pp. 153–243, at p. 154.
10 Hall, *The Oxford Companion*, p. 29.
11 S. Wasby, *The Supreme Court in the Federal Judicial System* (4th edn), Chicago, 1993, p. 357.
12 T. Marshall, *Public Opinion and the Supreme Court*, London and Boston, 1989, p.145.
13 *Ibid.*, p. 192.

Five—Advice and consent: the politics of Supreme Court appointments

---

In this chapter we analyse one of the most controversial aspects of the modern Supreme Court: the process of appointing new Justices. Amongst other things, we will explore such questions as who becomes a Supreme Court Justice and why? Who influences the selection of the Justices and how? And what effect does the selection process have upon the subsequent behaviour of the Justice once seated upon the Court? In short, we shall examine the power and politics of Supreme Court appointments.

The constitutional framework

The broad framework for the appointment of Supreme Court Justices is delineated in Article II, Section 2 of the Constitution. This states that the President 'shall nominate, and by and with the Advice and Consent of the Senate, shall appoint ... Judges of the Supreme Court'.

Like most constitutional clauses, Article II, Section 2 is open to varied and even conflicting interpretation, as we shall see shortly. Yet certain things are clear. First, it is important to note that there are two distinct phases of the process: *nomination* and *confirmation*. Nomination involves proposing someone for a seat on the Court, whereas confirmation entails approving or rejecting that nominee as a Justice of the Supreme Court.

Second, two institutions of the federal government are given a role in the process: the *President* and the *Senate*. Their roles, however, are different. The President has sole power over the nomination process, but the Senate has sole power over the confirmation process. In practice, this means that the President sends the name of a candidate for the Court to the Senate; and the Senate then decides whether to confirm or reject the President's nominee. If the nominee is confirmed, then he or she takes up the vacant seat on the Court. If rejected, however, then the President must begin the process again and propose a new nominee to the Senate.

This division of responsibilities and power reflects, of course, the broader commitment of the framers of the Constitution to the separation of governmental powers and to a system of checks and balances, both of which were aimed at ensuring that no single person or institution could acquire too much power. Thus it was the intention of the framers to prevent either the executive branch (the President) or the legislative branch (the Senate, but not in this case the House) from having sole control over the selection of Supreme Court Justices and thus from controlling the judicial branch (the Supreme Court).

At the Philadelphia Convention of 1787, the delegates had discussed a variety of proposals for the appointment of members of the Court. Some sought to give the power exclusively to the President, while others placed judicial selection solely in the hands of the legislative branch. Proponents of the former were fearful that the legislature would appoint Justices selected for crass political reasons or who were otherwise 'unfit' for the high bench. Those who favoured legislative selection, however, feared that an unconstrained President would simply appoint his acolytes to the Court, much as they believed George III had done in England.

The eventual plan to share power between the President and the Senate was thus a compromise, designed to allay the fears of both parties. It is important to note that the compromise allowed no role for the most democratic branch of the federal government, the House of Representatives. Clearly the framers were not convinced that those politicians chosen directly by the people were sufficiently responsible to be entrusted with the task of appointing the guardians of the Constitution.

Nevertheless, one major consequence of the division of power in the Appointments clause was to create the potential for conflict between the President and the Senate over the composition of the Court. And at different phases in history, that potential has become real, and none more so than in the present day.

Advice and consent

Conflict between President and Senate has in part turned on the meaning of 'Advice and Consent' in Article II, Section 2 of the Constitution. For nowhere does the Constitution suggest either what criteria should guide the President in his choice of nominee, or on what grounds the Senate should confirm or reject presidential nominees. Surprisingly, perhaps, there are no formal qualifications required for a

Supreme Court Justice – not even a law degree or prior judicial experience. As a result, the President and Senate were left entirely to their
own devices in deciding how to approach their joint power of Supreme
Court appointment.

The presidential school

Broadly speaking, two approaches emerged. The first might be termed
the *presidential school*. This holds that the President is the senior partner in the appointment process. This is indicated, it is said, by the fact
that the framers set out the method of appointment of Supreme Court
Justices in Article II of the Constitution, which deals with the powers
of the executive branch. Furthermore, by giving the President sole
power to nominate Justices, the logic of the Constitution is that
responsibility for the composition of the Court is entrusted primarily
to the executive branch.

The presidential school therefore concludes that the President is
free to nominate whoever he wishes and that his choice may be based
upon a variety of criteria, including the nominee's political, judicial
and philosophical views. The Senate, on the other hand, is more constrained. Its task in confirming or rejecting the President's nominee is
limited to ensuring that he or she is technically and temperamentally
qualified to be a Supreme Court Justice. Thus the Senate is entitled
to reject a nominee who has been shown to be dishonest or corrupt,
or who is merely a crony of the President, with no demonstrated
capacity for judicial tasks.

What the Senate may not do, however, is to reject a nominee for
political reasons: that is, for example, because it does not agree with
the nominee's political or judicial philosophy or simply because it disapproves of the President himself. In short, the presidential school
argues that the President is entitled to have people of his own choos-
ing on the Court, unless he selects someone who is manifestly unfit for
the task.[1]

The partnership school

A different view, however, is taken by what might be called the *partnership school*. This school sees the Senate and President as co-equals
in the Supreme Court appointments process, with each free to make
its decisions according to whatever criteria it deems appropriate.

Undoubtedly the main thrust of the partnership approach is to justify Senate consideration of presidential nominees on political grounds, as well as grounds of competence and fitness. Not only is the Senate free to do this as an independent, co-equal partner, but it is virtually obliged to do this by the fact that the President usually selects his nominees on political grounds.

This school does not suggest that the Senate should routinely reject presidential nominees on political grounds. This, after all, would be likely to bring the entire appointments process grinding to a halt: it is unreasonable and impracticable to expect a President not to nominate those of his own political party or ideological persuasion. However, where the Senate perceives a nominee's ideology as extreme or likely to take the Court in a new direction, then it is proper for the Senate to consider the political character and possible impact of the nominee. In short, the Senate is not obliged to show deference to the President when the nominee may cause significant changes in the judicial and political direction of the Court.[2]

The Senate's role in the appointments process: three Senators state differing views

Senator Orrin Hatch (R – Utah)

There are, undoubtedly, areas where Judge Breyer and I will disagree in our reading of the law. I do not expect to agree with any nominee, especially one chosen by a President of the other party, on every issue that will come before the judicial branch. But it has been my consistent belief that a President – and this President – is entitled to significant deference in selecting a Supreme Court Justice ... President Clinton and I are unlikely ever to agree on the person who ought to be nominated. But so long as a nominee is experienced in the law, is intelligent, has good character and temperament, and gives clear and convincing evidence of understanding the proper role of the judiciary in our system of government, I can support that nominee. *(Conservative Republican Senator Orrin Hatch stating his approach to Democrat President Bill Clinton's nomination of Stephen Breyer: Senate Judiciary Committee Hearings, 1994)*

Senator Dennis DeConcini (D – Arizona)

The advice and consent duty of the Senate is one of this body's most important constitutional powers. But this provision provides no immutable standard for Senators to look to when faced with the responsibility of voting on a Supreme Court nomination. I have often stated and believe that the Senate should give the President's nominee the benefit of the doubt. But this in no way means that we should confirm a nominee without thoroughly examining his or her qualifications. As the Senate does not expect the President to rubber stamp its legislation, the President should not expect Congress to rubber stamp his nominees.

A Supreme Court Justice is not a cabinet member whose job is to serve the President. It is not sufficient that the President agrees with the views of the nominee. The Senate has a right, indeed a constitutional obligation, to examine a nominee's competence, integrity, experience, and yes – his or her judicial philosophy. For the Supreme Court is undeniably a policymaker.

We have heard from groups who either oppose the nomination of Judge Thomas or have grave concerns in placing him on the country's highest court, including national groups representing the interests of women, Hispanics, African-Americans, and the elderly ... But I believe that Judge Thomas's opponents have the burden in persuading this Senator that Judge Thomas should not be confirmed. *(Moderate Democrat Senator Dennis DeConcini stating his approach to Republican President George Bush's nomination of Clarence Thomas: Senate Judiciary Committee Hearings, 1991)*

Senator Edward Kennedy (D – Mass.)

Today, the Senate begins one of the most important tasks entrusted to it under the Constitution: consideration of a nomination to the Supreme Court ... The Constitution itself is silent on what standard the Senate should apply in weighing a Supreme Court nomination ... [T]he Senate must make two inquiries. The first is a threshold issue: Does the nominee have the intelligence, integrity, and temperament to meet the responsibilities of a Supreme Court Justice?

But that is not the only inquiry. The Senate must also determine whether the nominee possesses a clear commitment to the fundamental values at the core of our constitutional democracy. In this second inquiry, the burden of proof rests with those who support a nomination ... If a Senator is left with substantial doubts about a nominee's dedication to these core values, our own constitutional responsibility requires us to oppose the nomination ...

Recent developments at the Supreme Court have increased the importance of this inquiry by the Senate. Over the past few years, the Court has retreated from its historic role in protecting civil rights and civil liberties. In case after case, the Court has adopted narrow and restrictive interpretations of important civil rights laws. The Senate is entitled to ensure that nominees to the Nation's highest court share Congress' view that these laws must be interpreted generously, to provide effective remedies to eliminate unfair discrimination in all its forms. *(Liberal Senator Edward Kennedy stating his approach to Republican President George Bush's nomination of David Souter: Senate Judiciary Committee Hearings, 1990).*

The statements from the three Senators above show that even within the Senate, there is no agreed view on exactly how the Senate should exercise its advice and consent power. Whereas Senator Hatch clearly sympathises with the *presidential school*, Senator Kennedy adheres vigorously to the *partnership school*. Senator DeConcini, however, places himself somewhere between the two.

Given the lack of specificity in the Constitution and the differing inclinations of Senators, it is not surprising that the history of Supreme Court appointments shows that, in practice, both schools of thought have been influential. If we now look in detail at how both Presidents and Senate have gone about their respective roles, we will see that while political factors loom large in the deliberations of both, senatorial deference to presidential selection is also a key feature.

Presidential nominations: major criteria

It is a commonplace observation that, through their power to nominate Justices of the Supreme Court, Presidents can influence the course of American politics long after they themselves have left office. Thus, President Nixon may have been forced to resign the presidency in disgrace in 1974, but his political influence lived on for at least a dozen years after that through his four appointments to the Court. Even today, his mark is still on the Court in the form of Chief Justice William Rehnquist, who was first placed on the Court as an Associate Justice by Nixon in 1971. Thus, while Presidents are limited to a maximum of eight years in office, their Supreme Court Justices may serve twenty-five years and more. If they choose wisely, Supreme Court appointments may prove to be a President's greatest political legacy. Unsurprisingly, therefore, most Presidents try to mould the Court in their own political image, a goal which leads them to apply certain criteria when selecting a nominee.

Judicial quality

It might be thought that the first criterion a President would apply in selecting a Supreme Court nominee would be judicial ability. After all, the Supreme Court is the nation's highest judicial body and is charged with the formidable responsibility of upholding the Constitution: it would seem to demand, therefore, Justices of the highest quality.

However, as we shall see below, Presidents usually place political criteria before judicial standards. Of course, the ideal nominee in the President's eyes is one who shares his own politics and yet who also commands high respect in legal circles. Such a nominee will not only hopefully fulfil the President's ideological expectations, but may also command support from the other Justices. Nevertheless, where no such ideal nominee exists, the President will usually sacrifice judicial brilliance for ideological compatibility and the prospects of a successful confirmation outcome.

It was noted above that Supreme Court Justices are formally required to have neither a law degree nor prior judicial experience. Yet there has always been an unwritten rule that nominees should possess a law degree, even if they have never pursued a legal career. Moreover, it is becoming increasingly common for nominees to have some lower federal court experience as a judge. Indeed, President Reagan consciously prepared candidates earmarked for nomination to the Supreme Court by appointing them to a federal judgeship: for example, Justice Scalia and the failed nominees Robert Bork and Douglas Ginsburg were all given stints on the DC federal court. President Bush did the same with Clarence Thomas.

The American Bar Association rating

Furthermore there is another informal factor which encourages the selection of nominees with prior judicial experience: the evaluation of candidates by the American Bar Association (ABA). The ABA is the nation's principal professional association for lawyers and it believes that its view of the judicial qualities of nominees should carry great weight in the confirmation process. In 1946 the ABA created a Standing Committee on the Federal Judiciary, which now rates nominees to the Court in one of three ways: *well qualified, qualified or not qualified.*

The American Bar Association rates Stephen Breyer

At the request of the administration, our committee investigated Judge Breyer's professional qualifications. Our investigation assessed Judge Breyer's integrity, his judicial temperament, and professional competence. Our work involved discussion with more than 500 persons, including Supreme Court Justices, Federal and State Court judges from all over the country, and practising lawyers throughout the United States. The committee members also interviewed law school professors, including constitutional law and Supreme Court scholars.

In addition, Judge Breyer's opinions were read by two reading groups ... Their reports were evaluated by members of our committee who also read Judge Breyer's opinions and his published writings on various legal subjects. Finally, Judge Breyer was interviewed by two members of our committee.

The Committee began its investigation of Judge Breyer on May 17, 1994, and completed its work on June 30, 1994. Based on our evaluation, we reported to the White House and to this committee that the standing committee is unanimously of the opinion that Judge Breyer is well qualified, the highest rating for a nominee to the Supreme Court of the United States. *(Written statement of the Standing Committee on the Federal Judiciary of the American Bar Association on federal court judge Stephen Breyer: Senate Judiciary Committee Hearings, 1994)*

Because the role of the Committee is informal, Presidents may choose the extent to which they submit nominees to its scrutiny. Many Presidents have submitted a list of possible nominees to the Committee, thus giving it considerable influence over the eventual selection. President Reagan, on the other hand, refused to do this, since he believed that the Committee was hostile to conservative nominees.

Regardless of whether they cooperate, however, there is no doubt that the ABA rating can affect a nominee's chances of confirmation. Thus, Robert Bork was damaged by being rated only 'qualified', as indeed was Clarence Thomas. On the other hand, a rating of 'well qualified' helped Anthony Kennedy to gain confirmation for the vacancy for which Bork had been intended.

Prior judicial experience

Traditionally, Republican Presidents have been more inclined that Democrats to select nominees with prior judicial experience. This stems from their desire to see Justices practise judicial restraint, something they believe is more likely when the Court is filled with those steeped in the legal tradition. Conversely, they distrust those with a mainly political background, since they fear that such nominees will continue to behave as politicians once on the Court.

Because Republicans have dominated the White House since 1968, all current members of the Court have some judicial experience, except one – Chief Justice Rehnquist. And he at least had relevant experience in that he served as Assistant Attorney General prior to his appointment as Associate Justice in 1971.

Whereas earlier Democrat Presidents tended to downplay judicial experience when selecting nominees, President Clinton appears to have fallen in line with Republican practice. Both Justices Ginsburg and Breyer had substantial judicial experience prior to their nomination. And it is beyond doubt that such experience is usually a positive factor in overcoming opposition to a nominee.

Yet it is possible that politicians with little or no judicial experience will be considered again in the future. After all President Clinton did seriously consider nominating former Democrat Senate Majority Leader George Mitchell and both Presidents Reagan and Bush considered Republican Senator Orrin Hatch of the Judiciary Committee. However, while politicians may bring valuable skills to the Court, they are also likely to have attracted more controversy than lower court judges. And in an era of difficult confirmation battles, judges continue to be a safer bet.

Party

An examination of the history of presidential nominations to the Supreme Court reveals one overwhelming fact: Presidents select nominees of their own party. In only a handful of almost 150 nominations to the Court has the President gone outside of his party for a Supreme Court nominee. This tradition was firmly established by George Washington who made fourteen nominations for the Court, every one of them a Federalist like himself.[3] His successors of all parties entrenched Washington's precedent so deeply that it was not until 1863 that a President successfully nominated a Justice who was not of his own party.[4] Even in this case, however, politics was the dominant consideration. Republican President Abraham Lincoln appointed the Democrat Stephen Field mainly because Field was an ardent Unionist. Thus the appointment was designed to strengthen bi-partisan support for Lincoln and the Union during the Civil War.

The most recent examples of cross-party selection date back to the Nixon administration (1969–74) and were similarly inspired by political manoeuvering. President Nixon had a 'Southern strategy' by which he hoped to woo Southern voters away from their traditional attachment to the Democratic party. He therefore nominated two Democrats, Clement Haynsworth of South Carolina (1969) and Lewis Powell of Virginia (1971). Both men were not only Southerners, but also inclined towards the President's desire for a more conservative Court.

There are two obvious reasons why Presidents pick nominees of their own party. First, there is the simple factor of patronage: when they capture the White House, Presidents of both parties are expected to reward their supporters with the spoils of office. Second, and even more important, party is a good guide to political and, Presidents hope, judicial orientation. As noted above, all Presidents seek to influence the Court's decisions through their power of appointment and party is one of the best indicators of ideological compatibility between President and nominee.

Ideology

Party may not, however, provide sufficient guidance to a president seeking to maximise his political influence over the Court. For some Presidents, the principal aim is to put a conservative or liberal Justice on the Court and they will therefore seek to assure themselves that nominees are in tune with their vision of judicial role and policy. Thus Franklin D. Roosevelt's initial appointments were driven by his desire to secure judicial approval of his liberal New Deal programme. He adopted the strategy, therefore, simply of nominating those who had already held political positions in which they had demonstrated their zeal for the New Deal. His first appointee was Democratic Senator Hugo Black, of Alabama, who had played a prominent role in promoting New Deal legislation; and his second was Stanley Reed, who Roosevelt had earlier made his Solicitor General.

More recently, President Reagan was determined to appoint conservatives who were willing to reverse the liberal decisions of the 1960s and 1970s. The Reagan White House therefore established elaborate procedures, including a specialist committee, for the ideological vetting of those considered possible nominees. The committee combed the judicial and political career of the candidates, read their published writings and questioned them on their views on specific constitutional questions. It was widely believed that, above all else, their position on the abortion issue was a 'litmus test' of whether they were ideologically qualified to be a Reagan appointee.

President Reagan certainly succeeded in placing judicial conservatives on the Court, Justice Antonin Scalia being the clearest example. However, his attempt to appoint Robert Bork, perceived as an extreme conservative, was defeated by the Senate.

Personal symbolism

A further factor which may enter into a President's calculations is a nominee's ability to provide symbolic representation on the Court to a particular section of American society.

Well into the twentieth century, the geographical origins of nominees was considered a significant factor. Presidents sought to ensure that all regions of the country felt an identity with the nation's highest court and, through it, with the Constitution. This was particularly true for regions which were distant from the East Coast centres of national power, the South and the West. President Franklin D. Roosevelt had to contend with this factor as late as 1939, when he nominated William O. Douglas. Roosevelt thought that geographical balance required him to put a Westerner on the Court. Douglas was indeed raised in Yakima, Washington, but had made his career in law and politics in the East. Only when politicians from the West assured the President that Douglas was a bona fide Westerner did Roosevelt proceed with the nomination.

The emphasis on geographical origins reflected the potential for sectional division within the Union. As geographical distinctiveness diminished in the mid-twentieth century, other bases for division came to the fore in regard to symbolic representation. In 1916, Louis Brandeis became the first Jewish Supreme Court Justice and thereby created the tradition of a 'Jewish seat' on the Court which lasted until 1969. Given a long tradition of anti-semitic sentiment in American life, it became important to demonstrate that Jews belonged in the highest circles of government, including on the body that was charged with ensuring the equal treatment of all citizens.

As anti-semitism faded as a concern, other racial considerations took their place. In 1967, President Lyndon Johnson put a symbolic seal on the civil rights 'revolution' by nominating the first African-American Justice, Thurgood Marshall. When Marshall retired in 1991, President Bush was careful to nominate another African-American to replace him, Clarence Thomas. And it is only a matter of time before a President nominates the first Hispanic-American to the Court.

Gender too became a factor in the wake of the women's rights movement of the 1960s and 1970s. President Reagan hoped to overcome some of his difficulty in attracting women voters by using his appointment powers to demonstrate that he was not hostile to sex equality: in 1981, he appointed the first woman to the Court, Sandra Day O'Connor.

Generally speaking, however, the factor of symbolic representation is subordinate to questions of ideology. President Reagan would not have nominated Justice O'Connor had she been a liberal and the same is true of President Bush's nomination of Clarence Thomas. In terms of the political return a President can expect from Supreme Court nominations, symbolic representation is a bonus, not the main reward. The ability to shape the Court is one's own political image remains the overriding goal.

Confirmability

We noted above that there is some disagreement over exactly what the Senate's role should be in the Supreme Court appointments process. Some argue for a vigorous and explicitly political Senate examination of presidential nominees, while others believe the senatorial role should be limited to ensuring that nominees merely meet minimal judicial standards. In fact, throughout most of American history, the Senate applied the latter criteria, though there were occasional bouts of politically-inspired senatorial truculence.

President Clinton's appointment of Justice Stephen Breyer in 1994 was the 113th successful nomination to the Court since 1789. This includes Associate Justices who were subsequently nominated to be Chief Justice. During the same period, twenty-eight nominations failed either because the Senate explicitly rejected them or because the Senate refused to act on the nomination, causing it to be withdrawn.[5]

Historically, therefore, the rejection rate is roughly one-in-five. However, until quite recently Senate rejection of Supreme Court nominees appeared to be a thing of the past. For between the confirmations of Edward White in 1894 and Thurgood Marshall in 1967, there were forty-five successful presidential nominations and just one rejection: that of John J. Parker in 1930. Moreover, the great majority of the nominees were confirmed without significant Senate opposition.

Since 1968, however, the picture has changed. Of eighteen nominations, three were rejected by Senate vote, one was withdrawn in the face of a Senate filibuster and yet another was withdrawn even before the nomination was made official. Moreover, in 1991, Justice Clarence Thomas came within a whisker of being rejected and two other nominations encountered significant Senate opposition. Eight of the last eighteen nominations have, therefore, been troubled. In short, whereas during the first two-thirds of the twentieth century, a President was virtually certain to have his Supreme Court nominees confirmed by the Senate, recent decades have seen the appointments process become much riskier (see Table 5.1).

Table 5.1 Supreme Court nominations since 1968

Year	Nominee	President	Senate action
1968	Abe Fortas*	Lyndon Johnson	Filibuster – *withdrawn*
1969	Warren Burger*	Richard Nixon	*Confirmed*, 74–3
1969	Clement Haynesworth	Richard Nixon	*Rejected*, 45–55
1970	G. Harrold Carswell	Richard Nixon	*Rejected*, 45–51
1970	Harry Blackmun	Richard Nixon	*Confirmed*, 94–0
1971	Lewis Powell	Richard Nixon	*Confirmed*, 89–1
1971	William Rehnquist	Richard Nixon	*Confirmed*, 68–26
1975	John Paul Stevens	Gerald Ford	*Confirmed*, 98–0
1981	Sandra Day O'Connor	Ronald Reagan	*Confirmed*, 99–0
1986	William Rehnquist*	Ronald Reagan	*Confirmed*, 65–33
1986	Antonin Scalia	Ronald Reagan	*Confirmed*, 98–0
1987	Robert Bork	Ronald Reagan	*Rejected*, 42–58
1987	Douglas Ginsburg	Ronald Reagan	*Withdrawn*
1987	Anthony Kennedy	Ronald Reagan	*Confirmed*, 97–0
1990	David Souter	George Bush	*Confirmed*, 90–9
1991	Clarence Thomas	George Bush	*Confirmed*, 52–48
1993	Ruth Bader Ginsburg	Bill Clinton	*Confirmed*, 96–3
1994	Stephen Breyer	Bill Clinton	*Confirmed*, 87–9

*Nomination as Chief Justice

The reasons for this new assertiveness by the Senate are not entirely clear. It may be simply that there has occurred a coincidence of particular factors which has produced a rash of problematic nominations. On the other hand, there is evidence to suggest that the Senate has significantly changed its approach to the confirmation process and that it does not intend to return to the passive role it played earlier this century. Indeed, it may be that the Senate has decided to adopt the partnership concept of its confirmation powers, including the right to reject presidential nominees on purely political grounds.

In fact, a combination of discrete and systemic factors appears to be at work. Certainly the allegations of sexual harassment against Clarence Thomas, the outspokenness of Robert Bork or the dismal judicial record of G. Harrold Carswell were unusual features of their nomination proceedings. Moreover, any argument that they were rejected for their conservative politics needs to explain why equally conservative nominees, such as Antonin Scalia or Anthony Kennedy, were confirmed unanimously in the Senate.

On the other hand, not only has the quantity of troubled nominations increased, but the entire nomination-confirmation process has undergone qualitative change. Before the 1960s, the Senate Judiciary Committee rarely required nominees to appear before it; and the Senate as a whole rarely bothered to record a vote on nominations. Today, however, nominees are required to appear before the Judiciary Committee for several days of questioning, usually carried live on television. In the expectation of hostile questioning, presidential aides now prepare nominees by holding simulated hearings beforehand. Nominees are alerted to the difficult questions they may expect and how they should answer or sidestep them.

Moreover, active opposition to a nominee can be expected not only from Senators but also from interest groups who band together to form a powerful lobby. They in turn will forge alliances not only with like-minded Senators, but also with law school professors and journalists. The result is that a nominee may face a broad, coordinated phalanx of opposition. Of course, the White House and its friends in the Senate will also be active in trying to produce a similar alliance in support of the nominee, so that Supreme Court appointment battles become a proxy war between the contending forces of American politics. This is what happened with both the Bork and Thomas nominations.

As Table 5.1 indicates, such battles still only materialise in a minority of cases. What, then, can explain the prevalence of confirmation struggles these days, but also their erratic occurrence? The first thing to note is that Supreme Court nominations have become more contentious simply because the Court now plays a more controversial role in American politics. From the 1950s onwards, the liberal judicial activism of the Warren and Burger Courts gave the Court a consistently high political profile. From the late 1970s onwards, conservative opposition to such activism raised that profile even higher. Almost inevitably, therefore, liberals and conservatives alike simply came to the realisation that Supreme Court nominations mattered more than ever before to the future political direction of the country.

A second factor behind the increased frequency of Senate opposition to presidential nominees is the tendency towards divided party control of the White House and the Senate. For with the exception of the Fortas nomination, all the troubled nominations shown in Table 5.1 occurred when a Republican President was confronted by a Democrat majority in the Senate. It should be noted at this point that, although only a simple majority of Senators is needed to confirm or reject a nominee, opposition from a sizeable minority can derail a nomination, as occurred with the filibuster that caused the Fortas nomination as Chief Justice to be withdrawn. Straightforward partisanship is thus an important part of the explanation of troubled nominations, sometimes even when the President's party has a majority in the Senate.

However, the fact remains that most nominees sail through the confirmation process, even when the Senate is in opposition hands. Clearly, therefore, Senators do not believe that they are entitled to reject nominees purely on political grounds. In other words, while they are more prepared today to be assertive, they still accept that the President is the senior partner in the appointments process and that he is entitled to nominate someone of his own political persuasion. The Senate, then, is poised somewhere between the presidential school and the partnership school of Supreme Court nominations. Put differently, the political balance of the Court and partisanship are necessary but not sufficient conditions of a nomination battle.

The vital ingredient, therefore, would appear to be a characteristic of the nominee which gives the Senate a reason – or, more likely, a pretext – for concluding that he or she is not fit to be a Justice of the Supreme Court. All the failed or difficult nominations since 1968 have involved such a conclusion, sometimes warranted, sometimes not. Rehnquist and Bork were alleged to be so extreme as to be outside the judicial mainstream of the country; Fortas and Haynesworth were vulnerable to charges of ethical violations; Carswell's judicial record was one of the worst in the country and he was also suspected of being a racist; Thomas was accused of sexual harassment; and Ginsburg admitted having smoked marijuana while a professor at Harvard.

A bitter Supreme Court battle: The nomination of Robert Bork, 1987

With the Supreme Court delicately balanced between liberals and conservatives, President Reagan made an ill-fated attempt to push the Court decisively to the right by nominating Robert Bork. Bork was well known for his trenchant views on liberal judicial activism and many of the Court's major progressive decisions of recent decades. Liberals responded, not always fairly, by painting Bork as an extremist bent on turning back the clock on civil liberties. Here, for example, is an excerpt from the statement made by leading liberal Senator Edward Kennedy on the day Bork's nomination was made known:

> Mr Bork should ... be rejected by the Senate because he stands for an extremist view of the Constitution and the role of the Supreme Court that would have placed him outside the mainstream of American constitutional jurisprudence in the 1960s, let alone the 1980s.
> Robert Bork's America is a land in which women would be forced into back-alley abortions, blacks would sit at segregated lunch counters, rogue police could break down citizens' doors in midnight raids, schoolchildren could not be taught about evolution, writers and artists would be censored at the whim of the government, and the doors of the Federal courts would be shut on the fingers of the millions of citizens for whom the judiciary is often the only protector of the individual rights that are at the heart of our democracy.
> President Reagan is still our President. But he should not be able to ... impose his reactionary vision of the Constitution on the Supreme Court and on the next generation of Americans. No justice would be better than this injustice.' *(Senator Edward Kennedy's statement in the Senate on the Bork nomination, 1 July 1987)*

Yet one might equally detect political motivations behind these confirmation battles. Fortas was at least in part a victim of the fact that he was nominated by a lame-duck Democrat President in an election year which promised to put a Republican in the White House. And to the Republican opposition to Fortas' elevation as Chief Justice was added Southern Democrats who disliked his part in the Warren Court's liberal jurisprudence. Even more clearly, Robert Bork was defeated by a moderate-liberal coalition in the Senate that feared he would tip an evenly balanced Court sharply to the right, especially on the abortion issue. An attempt was made to reconstruct the anti-Bork coalition in order to prevent Clarence Thomas's confirmation, but it foundered initially because no special issue could be found to use against him. Only when charges of sexual harassment emerged late in the day was Thomas's confirmation placed in jeopardy.

Thus, the Senate may often wish to oppose a nominee on political grounds, but it believes it cannot do so without some plausible special reason above and beyond mere politics. The balance of power, therefore, remains with the President.

Nevertheless, the mere *potential* for confirmation conflict has altered the appointments process. Presidents must now carefully screen possible nominees to ensure that they are confirmable: that is, that there is no political, judicial or character flaw which will provoke Senate opposition. The mere hint of such a flaw may persuade the President to look elsewhere for his nominee and to seek out candidates who are unobjectionable, even though perhaps bland.

The modern prototype of a Supreme Court nominee is David Souter. When President Bush was given his first opportunity to make a Supreme Court nomination, he decided to go for confirmability rather than ideology. Conservatives urged the President to nominate someone who could be relied upon to continue the Reaganite campaign to end and reverse liberal judicial activism. Bush wanted to satisfy the conservative wing of the Republican party, but faced with a Democratic majority in the Senate, he feared that such a nominee might be 'Borked'. He decided to play safe with his first nominee, therefore, but promised conservatives that he would nominate someone who met their criteria when the next vacancy occurred. Bush kept his word: while he nominated the moderate David Souter for the first vacancy, Clarence Thomas became his second nominee.

Dubbed the 'stealth candidate' when nominated by President Bush in 1990, Souter had no personal or professional controversy in his past and dealt with his Senate hearings by offering bland, unrevealing assurances to questioners from all political quarters. Souter was easily confirmed. Moreover, President Bush's instincts were proved correct when the Thomas nomination met with fearsome opposition and was only just confirmed.

Perhaps having observed and learned from the Bork and Thomas nominations, President Clinton appears to have had confirmability uppermost in mind when he nominated Ruth Bader Ginsburg and Stephen Breyer to the Court. Both were on the moderate-liberal wing of American politics and jurisprudence and both offered something to potential conservative critics: Ginsburg was critical of some aspects of *Roe v. Wade* and Breyer was seen as conservative on business regulation.

Some fear that a proliferation of 'stealth candidates' will lead to a mediocre Court deprived of brilliant, albeit controversial, intellects. Only time will tell. But it should be noted that a brilliant legal or political mind is no guarantee of success as a Supreme Court Justice, since success depends on far more than intellect. Thus, while Justice Scalia may well be the brightest member of the Rehnquist Court, he is not as influential as colleagues such as O'Connor or Kennedy who can muster more votes behind their opinions.

Characteristics of the Justices

What kinds of people end up being nominated by the President and confirmed by the Senate as Justices of the United States Supreme Court? As Table 5.2 suggests, they tend to come from the nation's elite. Even those not born to high status families, like Justice Thomas, have usually found their way into elite circles by the time they reach law school, if not before. Thus, all the current members of the Court attended prestigious universities, including five at Harvard alone.

From such an educational background, it is not surprising that all went on to build successful political and/or legal careers. Some Justices are selected almost wholly on the strength of their judicial record; but for most, their political activities are important, because it is these which bring them to the attention of senior politicians at the state or federal level. Thus although neither pursued what could be termed straight political careers, Justices Ginsburg and Breyer both established strong political contacts through their legal work. Justice Ginsburg acted as legal counsel to the Women's Rights Project of the American Civil Liberties Union in the 1970s and made her name arguing several gender equality cases before the Supreme Court. Justice Breyer was Chief Counsel to the Senate Judiciary Committee from 1979 to 1980, something which later helped to secure support from both Republican and Democrat members of that committee when he was nominated to the Court.

The elite nature of the Court is also reinforced by the fact that white males have had an almost exclusive grip on membership. As we saw above, the first non-white Justice, Thurgood Marshall, was not appointed until 1967 and the first woman, Sandra Day O'Connor, was not appointed until 1981. In fact, of the 108 persons to have served on the Court up until 1995, all but two have been men and all but two have been white. This may be changing gradually, but the day is still a long way off when the Justices of the Supreme Court will faithfully reflect the ethnic and gender composition of the American people.

Table 5.2 Profile of the Justices of the Supreme Court, 1995

Justice	Date of birth	Date/age at appointment	Family status	Law school	Political/ judicial career
Rehnquist, William H.	1/10/24	1971 (47)	Upper-middle	Stanford	Assistant Attorney General/ None
Stevens, John Paul	20/4/20	1975 (55)	Upper	Northwestern	None/ Judge, Fed. Ct of Appeals
O'Connor, Sandra Day	26/3/30	1981 (51)	Upper-middle	Stanford	State Senator/ Judge, Ariz. Ct of Appeals
Scalia, Antonin	11/3/36	1986 (50)	Middle	Harvard	Assistant Attorney General/ Judge, Fed. Ct of Appeals
Kennedy, Anthony	23/7/36	1987 (51)	Upper-middle	Harvard	None/ Judge, Fed. Ct of Appeals
Souter, David H	17/9/39	1990 (50)	Middle	Harvard	State Att.orney General/ Judge, Fed. Ct of Appeals
Thomas, Clarence	23/6/48	1991 (43)	Lower	Yale	Chair, Equal Employment Opportunity Commission/ Judge, Fed. Ct of Appeals
Ginsburg, Ruth Bader	15/3/33	1993 (60)	Middle	Harvard	None/ Judge, Fed. Ct of Appeals
Breyer, Stephen G.	15/8/38	1994 (56)	Upper-middle	Harvard	None/ Judge, Fed. Ct of Appeals

Source: L. Epstein, J. Segal, H. Spaeth and T. Walker, *The Supreme Court Complendium: Data, Decisions and Developments* Washington, D.C. 1994, pp. 180–273; information on Breyer from *CQ Weekly*, 14 May 1994, p. 1215.

Of course, there is no simple connection between a Justice's personal characteristics and his or her judicial orientation. Thus of the present Court, Justice Thomas comes from the least privileged background and yet is amongst the most conservative of its members. Justice Stevens, on the other hand, has the most privileged background of any current member, but is amongst the most liberal in his jurisprudence.

Supreme Court nominees are overwhelmingly middle-aged when selected. This reflects two basic facts. First nominees must have established themselves in their chosen career in order to demonstrate that they are worthy to sit on the Court. This usually means that most have at least reached their forties. In the twentieth century, the youngest nominee was William O. Douglas, selected at the age of forty by President Franklin D. Roosevelt. Pushing in the opposite direction, however, is the fact that Presidents would like their appointees to remain on the Court for many years, so few nominees over the age of sixty are chosen. Thus the average age of the present members of the Court at the time of their appointment was fifty-one.

In short, a typical Supreme Court Justice is a white, middle-aged male from a family of middle-class or higher status. He has been educated at one of the country's best universities and has built a successful political or judicial career, which has brought him to the attention of leading politicians at the state or federal level. These things qualify him to be a member of the Court. But it is important to remember that, ultimately, he was nominated because the President believed he was best qualified not so much to be a great judge, but to further the President's own political agenda. We turn next, then, to see how well the Justices fulfil their nominating Presidents' hopes.

Post-confirmation judicial behaviour

As we have seen, the entire process of appointing Supreme Court Justices is imbued with attempts to discover or predict the nominee's views on the great constitutional controversies of the day and on the role of the Court in the political process. Yet once confirmed by the Senate, the new Justice is free to decide cases however he or she pleases. A Supreme Court Justice is accountable to no one for her or his decisions and faces no re-election or re-appointment. He or she is on the Court for life, if so desired. As a nominee he or she may have expressed views about particular issues or past decisions, but is under no obligation to hold fast to those views as a member of the Court deciding an actual case. In short, Presidents have no guarantee that those they appoint to the Court will behave as expected.

There have been, moreover, Supreme Court Justices who have surprised and disappointed their appointing President. The most famous example is that of Chief Justice Earl Warren, appointed by Republican President Eisenhower in 1953. Eisenhower was a moderate conservative and was looking for someone of a similar persuasion to become Chief Justice. Warren had been a moderate Republican Governor of California and had been the party's vice-presidential candidate in 1948. Eisenhower knew Warren personally and apparently had few doubts about naming him Chief Justice.

Within a year of taking office, however, Warren had begun a liberal crusade on the Court that was to last until his resignation in 1969. During that time, Warren launched a liberal transformation of constitutional law in matters such as race segregation, the rights of those accused of crime and legislative reapportionment. Moreover, Warren and his activist colleagues dramatically altered the role of the Court in the governmental process, making it a dynamic and positive force for social change. While liberals responded to the Warren Court's innovations with delight, Eisenhower was appalled. Nothing had been further from his mind when he had nominated Warren to the Court.

Eisenhower was also greatly disappointed by another of his appointees, William Brennan. Brennan was, admittedly, a Democrat but his reputation was that of a moderate liberal and a first-rate judge. Yet Brennan soon formed a close alliance with Warren and actually assumed leadership of the liberal-activist wing of the Court after Warren's retirement. It comes as no surprise, then, that when Eisenhower was asked if he had made any mistakes as President, he replied: 'Yes, two, and they are both sitting on the Supreme Court.'[6]

However, the occasional disappointment experienced by Presidents should not mask the fact that, generally, they get what they hoped for from their Supreme Court appointments. This does not mean that their appointees vote in every case in the way the President would have liked, or that Justices fit exactly into the ideological position on the Court intended by the President. Nevertheless, by large and large, if a President decides to make an ideological appointment to the Court, and chooses his nominee carefully, then he will usually find that his appointee fulfils his basic expectations.

Thus President Franklin D. Roosevelt wanted a liberal Court which, above all, would give Constitutional blessing to the New Deal and that is what he got. Presidents Kennedy and Johnson also wanted liberals on the Court, especially in the area of civil rights and liberties, and their appointees did not let them down. Richard Nixon, however, obtained only mixed results. While William Rehnquist turned out to

THE POLITICS OF APPOINTMENTS

be a true conservative, Warren Burger and Lewis Powell adopted moderate positions on most issues. Most disappointing of all, from Nixon's point of view, Harry Blackmun gradually became one of the Court's most liberal members.

If we look at the Court today, however, we find that all its members are cast more or less in their appointing President's image. The Reagan appointees – O'Connor, Rehnquist as Chief Justice, Scalia and Kennedy – are all conservatives, although O'Connor and Kennedy have not always proved willing to go as far as Reagan wanted in reversing the liberal decisions of the Warren and Burger Courts.

President Bush appointed David Souter as a moderate who could easily be confirmed and that has been the general tenor of Souter's votes, although he is more liberal on some social issues than conservatives would like. Clarence Thomas, on the other hand, is a delight for conservatives and regularly lines up with Justice Scalia and Chief Justice Rehnquist to form the Court's conservative core.

President Clinton aimed to appoint moderate liberals and, at least in their early years on the Court, Justices Ginsburg and Breyer fitted that mould. That leaves Justice Stevens, appointed by President Ford in 1975. Ford selected Stevens as a respected, moderate judge and, although sometimes described as idiosyncratic, Stevens can reasonably be classified as a moderate liberal.

Overall, then, Justices Souter and Stevens are somewhat more liberal than their appointing Presidents hoped and Justices O'Connor and Kennedy are somewhat less activist than President Reagan had hoped. Nevertheless, the current Supreme Court clearly bears the political imprint of the Presidents who appointed its members. Thus, while Presidents may not get everything they want when they make Supreme Court appointments – and may sometimes get a very nasty surprise – they usually get a very satisfactory political return on their judicial investments.

Summary

The power to appoint new Supreme Court Justices is one shared by the President and the Senate. Despite the growing politicisation of the appointment process and the increasing assertiveness of the Senate, however, the President stiil retains the upper hand. If he chooses his nominee carefully and avoids controversy, the President should be able to appoint someone of his own party and ideology. And unless he is unlucky, that Supreme Court Justice will carry the flag for the President's broad views long after he has left the White House.

Notes

1 N. Vieira and L. Gross, 'The Appointments Clause: Judge Bork and the Role of Ideology in Judicial Confirmations', *The Journal of Legal History*, XI, 1990, pp. 311_52.

2 L. Tribe, *God Save This Honorable Court: How the Choice of Supreme Court Justices Shapes Our History*, New York, 1985, pp. 128–34.

3 L. Epstein J. Segal, H. Spaeth and T. Walker, *The Supreme Court Compendium: Data, Decisions, and Developments*, Washington, D.C., 1994, Table 4–11, pp. 274–82. It should be noted that different authors may give slightly different totals for the number of nominations, depending on whether they include those which were withdrawn by the President before any senatorial action. Unless otherwise indicated, I include all presidential nominees in the figures given here.

4 President John Tyler, nominally a Whig, successfully nominated the Democrat Samuel Nelson to the Court in 1845. By this time, however, Tyler had broken with his party and effectively was operating as a Democrat.

5 H. Abraham, *Justices and Presidents* (3rd edn), New York, 1992, p. 39. A few others have also failed to make it to the Court for various reasons not involving Senate deliberation. For example, in 1987 President Reagan announced that he would nominate Douglas Ginsburg, but the nomination never officially took place: Ginsburg's name was quickly withdrawn when it was revealed that he had smoked marijuana as an adult.

6 Abraham, *Justices and Presidents*, p. 266.

Six—The power of the Supreme Court: constraints, compliance and impact

Decisions of the Supreme Court are not self-executing. The Court relies on other branches of government to enforce its decisions, but such compliance may not be readily forthcoming. In this chapter we examine the politics of compliance and resistance in implementing Supreme Court decisions. And we make an assessment of the impact of the Court's decisions on American society and politics and thus its power.

The formal position

In no. 78 of *The Federalist Papers* (Chapter Two, page 48), Alexander Hamilton predicted that the Court would be the weakest of the three branches of the federal government. In part, this was because the Court had no means of enforcing its decisions and consequently had to rely upon the President or state governments to ensure compliance with them. Indeed, even more fundamentally, the Court's very power and legitimacy depends upon the voluntary recognition of its authority by the other branches of government.

Formally, of course, all branches of government are honour-bound to comply with Supreme Court decisions. The President, for example, swears an oath of office in which he pledges to uphold the Constitution. And, formally at least, that means interpretations of the Constitution by the Supreme Court. Moreover, the Court is due respect as a co-equal branch of the federal government, with its own area of competence and expertise.

None of this means, however, that federal and state authorities are obliged passively to accept whatever the Court decides. As we saw in Chapter Three, there are formal mechanisms by which Congress can seek to overturn judicial interpretations of the Constitution of which they disapprove. Most obviously, Congress can initiate the process of constitutional amendment to reverse a Supreme Court decision. Congress can also remove the appellate jurisdiction of the Court over any issue it chooses, be it abortion, affirmative action or gay rights.

There are also less direct means of attacking the Court. Congress may vary the number of Justices who sit on the Court and the President and Senate can, as we saw in the previous chapter, use their joint powers of appointment to alter the Court's future political direction.

These formal obligations of compliance and instruments of resistance do not, however, capture the political realities of the enforcement of judicial decisions and policies. One reason is that that the aforementioned means of reversing Court decisions are rarely employed successfully. Thus the Constitution has only been amended four times specifically to overturn Supreme Court decisions and the appellate jurisdiction of the Court has only been curtailed once. Moreover, the number of Justices has been fixed at nine since 1869. And while the appointments process is heavily infused with political considerations, it provides no guarantee that a specific Court decision or policy will eventually be reversed.

Some of these formal mechanisms are, however, mobilised by opponents of particular Court decisions in order to bring added pressure on the Justices to reconsider or tone down a controversial policy. There have been dozens of proposed constitutional amendments and withdrawals of appellate jurisdiction aimed at the Court's decisions on abortion and school prayer, for example. But given the very poor likelihood that such measures will actually be passed, they are usually best viewed as part of the wider 'guerilla warfare' which is often waged against controversial decisions by the Court.

The political realities of compliance and resistance

The theory of judicial supremacy in matters of constitutional interpretation suggests that the Supreme Court has the final word on the meaning of the Constitution and the policies it mandates. Political reality, however, suggests otherwise.

We have seen that it is the political and social environment of the Court that provides it with its agenda. More precisely, it is the attitudes, beliefs and actions of legislatures, executive branches, interest groups, legal scholars and citizens which form the substance of Supreme Court cases. And given that these cases involve political and legal disputes, sometimes of a passionate nature, it defies common sense to suppose that when the Supreme Court issues its decision the conflict is thereby settled. Indeed, just as political activists turn to the Court when they have lost out in the legislative arena, those unsuccessful before the Court may well turn to legislative or executive branch action as a means of resisting judicial decisions.

Supreme Court decisions and policies, therefore, far from being final, are often simply one element in what Louis Fisher calls 'constitutional dialogues'.[1] This is a useful term to describe the continuous cycles of interaction between the Court and other political forces and institutions before a matter of constitutional interpretation is settled as political fact.

One should not, however, be misled by the use of the word 'dialogue' into believing that such interaction is always a civilised process of rational debate. Certainly on some issues it involves a bitter battle of wills and power. And it often begins with the refusal of the President, the Congress or the States to comply with the Court's decision.

Presidential non-compliance

What common sense suggests, history confirms. In fact, right from the very start of the practice of judicial review, the authority of the Court's decisions has been denied and resisted. This is true even of the President of the United States, the person with ultimate responsibility for enforcing the Court's decisions. Thus, as we saw in Chapter Two, even before the Court issued its landmark decision in *Marbury v. Madison* (1803), President Jefferson made it public that he would not accept any ruling that ordered him to appoint William Marbury as a Justice of the Peace. Even more famously, perhaps, the Indian-hating President Andrew Jackson refused to respect the Court's decision in *Worcester v. Georgia* (1832) upholding the sovereignty of the Cherokee Nation, allegedly saying, 'John Marshall has made his decision, now let him enforce it'. Outright defiance of Court decisions by the President is merely the most blatant form of resistance to judicial authority, however. Presidents have also mounted less direct, if equally lethal, attacks upon the Court's decisions. Undoubtedly the most determined of these was President Franklin D. Roosevelt's so-called 'Court-packing plan' of 1937, that we examined in Chapter Two.

Another form of presidential resistance is the public campaign to 'negotiate' or 'debate' a decision by the Court. The President may be seeking to influence the Justices directly by asking them to consider certain arguments; or he may be seeking to alter the political and legal climate in which the Court operates. Either way, the executive branch is trying to persuade the Court to modify or reverse its position.

One interesting example of an attempt at presidential negotiation with the Court occurred over the issue of busing during the adminstration of President Richard Nixon. Frustrated by the refusal of state authorities to integrate their schools in the light of the *Brown* decision, lower federal courts ordered many of them to bus white children to black schools and vice versa. Sometimes the bus journeys were long and this added just another source of opposition to the integration of America's schools. Nevertheless, the Supreme Court unanimously approved the principle of busing in *Swann v. Charlotte-Mecklenburg Board of Education* (1971).

Busing quickly became a hot political issue. Various measures were introduced in Congress to undermine or prohibit busing plans, as well as legislation withdrawing the appellate jurisdiction of the Supreme Court over the issue. And on 17 March 1972, a year in which President Nixon was seeking re-election, he sent a message to Congress requesting legislation to impose a moratorium on new busing orders. The proposed Student Transportation Moratorium Act of 1972 was intended to give Congress the time to develop national statutory guidelines for the implementation of school desegregation orders. It was also intended, of course, to win Nixon the votes of the predominantly working- and middle-class parents whose children attended public schools. But his message to Congress was also a carefully worded appeal to the Supreme Court to halt its busing policy and allow other branches of government a voice in determining desegregation plans.

Nixon's message avoided an attack on the Supreme Court itself, preferring to focus on the uncertainties created by variations in the many lower federal court orders that had been issued. But he did remind the Court that it was neither proper nor wise for it to assume sole responsibility for desegregation policy.

President Nixon's message to Congress on busing, March 1972

The Congress has both the Constitutional authority and a special capability to debate and define new methods for implementing Constitutional principles. And the educational, financial and social complexities of this issue are not, and are not properly, susceptible of solution by individual courts alone or even by the Supreme Court alone

...

This is not a time for the courts to plunge ahead at full speed

...

It has become abundantly clear, from the debates in the Congress and from the upwelling of sentiment in the country, that some action will be taken to limit the scope of busing orders. It is in the interests of everyone – black and white, children and parents, school administrators and local officials, the courts, the Congress and the executive branch, and not least in the interest of consistency in Federal policy – that while this matter is being considered by the Congress we not speed further along a course that is likely to be changed.

What the Nixon administration did on the particular policy of busing, the second Reagan administration (1985–89) did on the role and methods of the Court in general. The campaign was led by the Attorney General, Edwin Meese. Meese helped to stimulate a national debate over constitutional interpretation as he strongly urged the Court to return to the days when its aim was to discover the original intent behind any given clause of the Constitution. More specifically, he called for an end to the use of constitutional interpretation as a means of advancing the cause of social reform.

Address by Attorney General Edwin Meese on constitutional interpretation, July 1985

In recent decades, many have come to view the Constitution – more accurately, part of the Constitution, provisions of the Bill of Rights, and the Fourteenth Amendment – as a charter for judicial activism on behalf of various constituencies. Those who hold this view have often lacked demonstrable textual or historical support for their conclusions. Instead they have 'grounded' their rulings in appeals to social theories, to moral philosophies or personal notions of human dignity, or to 'penumbras', somehow emanating ghostlike from various provisions ... in the Bill of Rights. The problem with this approach ... is not that it is bad constitutional law, but that it is not constitutional law in any meaningful sense at all.

Whether and to what extent such forms of non-compliance with Court decisions are likely to succeed is debatable. Certainly in the case of Nixon's resistance to busing, one could point to the decision of the Court in *Milliken v. Bradley* (1974) where the Court declined to extend the scope of busing remedies to include school districts with no history of segregative practices. However, it is not possible to tell whether presidential opposition was an important factor in that decision. It is

perfectly plausible that the Court could have reached the same conclusion purely on grounds of legal reasoning. Or alternatively, it might
be that the Justices were more concerned about popular resistance to
busing than they were about presidential criticism.

All that can be said, therefore, is that presidential resistance to
Supreme Court decisions does occur and that it is an important factor
to be considered by the Court when it next comes to consider the relevant issue. This is particularly true, of course, when the presidency
is not the sole source of resistance to the Court.

Congressional non-compliance

For the President to resist a Supreme Court decision, he has the
option of simply doing nothing. Congress, however, must act. Nevertheless, as noted above, there are a number of methods available to
Congress by which they can undermine Court-ordered policies.

We have already seen that Congress rarely invokes with success the
process of constitutional amendment to overturn a Court decision
based on constitutional interpretation. Yet despite the difficulties of
securing the required two-thirds majority of both the House of Representatives and the Senate, members of Congress frequently resort to
this device to express their anger at the Court's decisions. Some do
come close to success. Following the Court's reapportionment decisions
of the 1960s, for example, Senator Everett Dirksen's proposed amendment to allow States to apportion one of their legislative chambers on
some other basis than population only fell two votes short in the Senate. And the persistent attempts to overcome the Court's ban on school
prayer may succeed one day.

**Constitutional amendments reversing Supreme Court
decisions**

Eleventh Amendment (ratified 1795)
Overturned *Chisholm v. Georgia* (1793) which upheld the right of a
citizen of one State to bring a suit against another State under the
original jurisdiction of the Supreme Court. Congress was motivated
primarily by the fear that *Chisholm* would undermine state sovereignty.

Thirteenth Amendment (ratified 1865)
Overturned *Dred Scott v. Sandford* (1857) which had upheld the

constitutionality of slavery. The Thirteenth Amendment was, in effect, the product of the defeat of the Confederacy in the Civil War. The Fourteenth and Fifteenth Amendments (ratified 1865 and 1870) also guaranteed rights which were denied former slaves in *Dred Scott*.

Sixteenth Amendment (ratified 1913)
Overturned *Pollock v. Farmers' Loan and Trust Co.* (1895) declaring a federal income tax unconstitutional. Congress was motivated both by the need to raise revenue to fund the rapidly expanding activities of the federal government and by the desire to counter the gross disparities of income produced by industrialisation.

Twenty-Sixth Amendment (ratified 1971)
Overturned *Oregon v. Mitchell* (1970) which declared that Congress did not have the right to establish a voting age of eighteen in state and local elections. Congress was motivated primarily by the anomaly produced in *Mitchell*, whereby the voting age in federal elections was lowered to eighteen but remained at twenty-one in States which did not wish to change their laws.

The frequency of congressional proposals for constitutional amendments compared with the near-certainty of their failure suggests that Congress uses such proposals for ulterior purposes. One is simply to express symbolic and public disapproval of a decision. This is particularly likely when members of Congress wish to reflect the hostility of the electorate or particular interest groups to the Court.

On the other hand, proposals for constitutional amendment may also be just one weapon employed in a broader campaign against an unpopular decision. When the Court produces a decision which offends the public or powerful sections of it, there may well result a long-term campaign to force the Court to retreat. Examples of such campaigns in the modern era include abortion, school prayer and desecration of the American Flag. In these campaigns, Congress uses every means at its disposal in order to put pressure on the Court. And while the Justices are extremely unlikely to reverse a decision they have made recently, the campaign may well pay off in time, when the Court's personnel has been changed.

Another weapon employed by the Congress against the Court is symbolic legislation. Legislation is symbolic in this context because statutes are inferior to the Constitution and cannot be used to overturn judicial interpretations of the Constitution. In these instances, then, Congress is once again demonstrating to the public and interest groups its hostility to judicial policies and thereby symbolically denying them legitimacy. A recent illustration occurred over flag-burning. In *Texas v. Johnson* (1989), the Court ruled that the First Amendment protected the right to burn the Stars and Stripes as part of a political protest. The decision was deeply offensive to most Americans and Congress responded by passing the Flag Protection Act of 1989, making it a federal offence to damage or burn the Flag. It was quite inevitable that the Court would not abandon its First Amendment reasoning and the Act was duly declared unconstitutional in *US v. Eichman* (1990). The Justices were thus not intimidated into making a retreat over flag-burning, but they were served notice that their decisions lacked government support. And since the power and prestige of the Court depend upon the voluntary recognition of its authority by others, the Flag Protection Act can be read as a warning not to go too far too often.

If direct contradictory legislation and proposed constitutional amendments are essentially symbolic demonstrations of disapproval of Court decisions, the Congress has other, more effective means of attacking Court policies. This involves legislation in the form of regulations governing the implementation of judicial policies. While these may not reverse the Court's decision, they can go a long way in undermining them.

As we shall see below, the abortion controversy reveals many examples of resistance to judicial policy. One of these involved Congress forbidding the expenditure of federal funds on virtually all kinds of abortions for women who normally depend on federal funds for health care. The so-called Hyde Amendment was first passed in 1976 and has been re-passed in one form or another every year since. Of course, such measures as the Hyde Amendment are subject to judicial review, but when enacted as part of a determined campaign against the Court's decisions, they may persuade the Justices to 'compromise' with their opponents.

There is also the possibility that Congress will combine with the President to ignore a Court decision. The outstanding example is the so-called 'legislative veto', which the Court declared unconstitutional in 1983 in *Immigration and Naturalization Service v. Chadha* (see also Chapter One). The legislative veto was a short-cut device which allowed Congress to make broad delegations of power to the President, but to retain a veto over specific exercises of those powers without having to go through the lengthy process of actually passing a new law. It had been built into hundreds of laws since it was first used in the 1930s, being a particularly useful device for overseeing the decisions of executive branch agencies. In *Chadha*, however, the Court ruled it unconstitutional on the grounds that as the veto was legislative in character, it had to conform to the usual process of enacting legislation.

However, both the Congress and successive Presidents have considered the legislative veto too useful to dispense with. As a result, Congress has continued to pass, and Presidents continued to sign, bills which include one form of legislative veto or another. Indeed, in the first three years after *Chadha* alone, some 102 legislative vetoes were introduced into twenty-four different statutes.[2] The Court may thus have had constitutional logic on its side, but its decision had gone too far in disrupting relations between Congress and the presidency. They simply ignored the Court, therefore, and there is nothing that the Court can do about it.

State non-compliance

By far the great majority of Supreme Court decisions declaring laws unconstitutional involve state, rather than federal, legislation. And combined with the fact that States are fiercely jealous of their sovereign rights, this means that the most frequent and determined examples of non-compliance emanate from the States.

Undoubtedly the most infamous instance of state non-compliance occurred as a result of the Court's desegregation decisions. Promising 'massive resistance' to *Brown v. Board of Education*, state legislatures employed a variety of devices to delay desegregation. Such was their success until the rest of the federal government stepped in that the episode provides a graphic illustration of what a weak hand the Supreme Court has to play when voluntary compliance is not forthcoming.

Table 6.1 shows the rate of compliance with *Brown* in the South and Border States, as measured by the number of black children attending elementary and secondary schools with whites. Non-compliance with *Brown* was almost total in the South, whereas the Border States were far less resistant. In consequence, ten years after *Brown* was decided, just 1.2 per cent of black children in the South attended desegregated schools, compared with 54.8 per cent in the Border States. Even allowing for the fact that the Border States started from a higher base, the difference is very instructive.

Table 6.1 The pace and extent of compliance with *Brown v. Board of Education* (percentage and number of black children in the South and Border States attending public schools with white children)

Year	South		Border	
	per cent	number	per cent	number
1954–5	0.001	23	n.a.	n.a.
1955–6	0.12	2,782	n.a.	n.a.
1956–7	0.14	3,514	39.6	106,878
1957–8	0.15	3,829	41.4	127,677
1958–9	0.13	3,456	44.4	142,352
1959–60	0.16	4,216	45.4	191.114
1960–1	0.16	4,308	49.0	212,895
1961–2	0.24	6,725	52.5	240,226
1962–3	0.45	12,868	51.8	251,797
1963–4	1.2	34,105	54.8	281,731

States in the South initially simply refused to implement *Brown* and then resorted to measures such as closing down public schools rather than integrating them. White crowds intimidated black schoolchildren who tried to attend formerly segregated schools and state governors refused to assure their access. When the federal authorities stepped in to enforce desegregation, white parents took their children out of the public school system. Only when the federal government enacted legislation that would impose severe financial penalties on States which did not comply did desegregation really take effect in the South.

On other occasions, when the Court has left the States with some discretion, they have used it to reject judicial policies. Thus when the Court declared all existing state death penalty laws unconstitutional in *Furman v. Georgia* (1972), most observers thought that capital punishment would never be seen again in the United States. But the Court had not said that the death penalty was unconstitutional in all circumstances and States responded rapidly by enacting new capital laws which apparently overcame the *Furman* objections. Fifteen States actually introduced mandatory capital punishment for certain types of murder. Such was the strength of state feeling on the matter that the Court made a palpable retreat in *Gregg v. Georgia* (1976) and has allowed States ever greater control of death penalty policy ever since. Today, fully thirty-eight States operate capital punishment. Moreover, in 1995 there were thirty-six executions and this in spite of Chief Justice Burger's statement in 1972 that 'There will never be another execution in this country.'[3]

The causes of non-compliance

It is abundantly clear that non-compliance with Supreme Court decisions is a significant feature of judicial review. It is necessary to inquire, therefore, into the conditions that are likely to give rise to a serious effort to thwart the Court.

Perhaps the first point to note is that there is no causal connection between the plausibility of the Court's interpretation of the Constitution and the degree of compliance. The Court has, on numerous occasions, made decisions which have proved wholly acceptable to other branches of government and the public, yet which have been based on dubious readings of the Constitution. Thus the Court's invention of a right to privacy in *Griswold v. Connecticut* (1965) barely caused a flutter outside of academic circles, simply because the Connecticut anti-contraception law struck down there was, as Justice Stewart said, 'uncommonly silly' (see also Chapter One).

It is then the substantive result or policy that renders a Supreme Court decision liable to negative reaction and non-compliance. To be sure, weak constitutional reasoning may be used as an additional stick with which to beat an unpopular decision, but it is never the fundamental cause of that unpopularity. The simple fact is that the public and most politicians are rarely even aware of the reasoning behind a decision, never mind animated by it. A comparison of the 'right to privacy' rationale in the contraception and abortion cases is instructive in this respect. While *Roe v. Wade* (1973) relied heavily on the *Griswold* logic, it nevertheless kicked off the most widespread and sustained opposition to a Supreme Court decision in modern times.

Having said that the unpopularity of the policy element of a Court decision is the key to non-compliance, however, it is not clear why some unpopular decisions stimulate active resistance while others do not. And here it is important to define exactly what we mean by 'unpopular'. There are three distinct groups whose approval or disapproval of a Court decision may prove decisive. First, other branches of government, including the President, Congress and state governments. Second, interest groups. And third, the general public. Which of these, either alone or in combination, are responsible for launching significant campaigns of non-compliance?

Unfortunately, there is no clear-cut answer to this. For the evidence suggests that the pattern of non-compliance varies with the issue. Take, for example, the non-compliance with the Court's ruling in *Chadha* (1983). The legislative veto was a matter of no interest to the general public, yet the President and Congress simply refused to accept the Court's edict. Similarly, the Court's reapportionment decisions aroused no great popular hostility, yet legislators came close to reversing them through constitutional amendment. In neither of these instances, moreover, was there a significant role played by interest groups. It is reasonable to conclude, therefore, that the Court runs a risk of non-compliance when its decisions adversely affect the traditional political arrangements of other branches of government. While the Court may still prevail, as in the reapportionment cases, it also suggests that the Court must tread carefully when it intervenes in the 'internal' affairs of other government institutions.

It is when the Court issues controversial decisions directly affecting society as a whole, however, that its authority is most likely to be challenged. Indeed, one of the reasons why non-compliance is a far more frequent phenomenon in recent decades is simply the nature of the Court's contemporary agenda. As we saw in Chapter One, the Court's contemporary agenda contains a major element of social issues, such as race and gender relations, sexual privacy and autonomy, religious values and crime and punishment. These cases affect the everyday lives of most Americans, be it through their jobs, their neighbourhoods, their families, their schools or their personal lives. Quite simply, these Supreme Court decisions are far more obviously salient to most Americans than previous Court agendas dealing with the economic liberties of corporations and individuals.

Nevertheless, it is not necessary for there to be a majority of the public opposed to a Court decision in order for it to become the object of resistance and non-compliance. The social issues on the Court's contemporary agenda are highly divisive ones which reflect the 'culture wars' which have raged in the United States since the 1960s. These wars not only divide the public but also pit interest groups against each other in the political arena. For a Supreme Court decision to raise the spectre of a campaign of non-compliance, therefore, it may only be necessary that it offend a significant portion of the public and 'representative' interest groups.

The public and interest groups may mount autonomous non-compliance activities. White Southerners barring the entrances of schools to black schoolchildren or pro-life demonstrators preventing access to abortion clinics provide notable examples. However, if non-compliance is to succeed, it is usually necessary for politicians to become involved. Politicians, after all, have their hands on the levers of power that can force the Court to retreat or compromise. And politicians *will* become involved either if they feel strongly about the issues themselves or, more likely, if they can thereby represent constituencies whose votes and money they hope to attract in subsequent elections. In other words, leading a campaign against an unpopular Supreme Court decision can offer substantial electoral advantages to both state and national politicians.

Ultimately, then, the key ingredients of a non-compliance campaign are the vested interests of other branches of government, the passions of interest groups, the disapproval of significant sections of the public and the beliefs and electoral strategies of politicians. The more of these that are aroused, and the greater the intensity of that arousal, the more the Court's decision is likely to face serious non-compliance.

However, even when non-compliance does take place, this does not necessarily presage a judicial defeat. For the Court may also have its own constituents who mount a counter-campaign to defend its decision. If we examine the aftermath of the Court's great abortion rights decision, we can see how rival campaigns can determine the degree of compliance with, and impact of, a controversial Court policy.

Abortion: A case study of compliance and impact

Roe v. Wade (1973) created an apparent revolution in abortion rights. Before the Court stepped in, States had always been considered sovereign over the issue. And even after the liberalising campaigns of the 1960s, most still had very strict controls over abortion, usually only allowing it when there would otherwise be a serious threat to the mother's life or health.

In 1973, then, the Supreme Court nationalised basic abortion policy and did so upon a very liberal basis. States could not ban abortion until the last three months of pregnancy and only then if there was no serious threat to the mother's health or life. In the second three months of pregnancy, the States were permitted only to regulate abortion procedures, while in the first three months, states had no powers whatsoever.

The decision was unmistakably a great victory for those who

believed in liberal abortion, particularly those who argued that only the kind of reproductive autonomy initiated by the Court could free women to play an equal role with men in society.

Inevitably, it also made enemies. Many States were simply angry that yet another area of their policy competence had been taken away by the federal judiciary. Equally importantly, the decision offended the moral sensibilities of many Americans who had not until 1973 paid much attention to abortion rights or politics in general. Before *Roe*, opposition to abortion rights had come mainly from the Catholic Church. Now, however, a popular movement developed to oppose abortion rights. These new activists were mainly those whose lifestyles were based on traditional family arrangements and values. They tended to be middle- and working-class married women with children, who did not work outside the home, had not been to college and were active Christians.[4] While they had not been antagonised by the medical arguments for limited abortion abortion rights, they were shocked into action by the *Roe* policy which went much further. They perceived *Roe* as sanctioning 'abortion on demand' and thereby saw it as a threat to the traditional family, traditional morality and their own social status.

They saw themselves as campaigning to stop the 'murder' of 'innocent lives' and described their actions and policies as 'pro-life'. They became the foot-soldiers in groups such as the National Right to Life Committee (NLRC), the League for Infants, Fetuses, and the Elderly (LIFE), and Operation Rescue. Together with sympathetic national and local politicians, they were to use every avenue of political action to resist, undermine and overthrow *Roe v. Wade*.

It should be emphasised at this point that *Roe* did not encounter majoritarian opposition amongst the public. Table 6.2 indicates initial and continuing support for *Roe* by most Americans, although the picture may be distorted by the particular phrasing of the question by pollsters.

The figures of support for *Roe* may be boosted by reverence for the Court as an institution. Table 6.3, however, indicates that on abortion policy itself, substantial if not always majoritarian support exists for the *Roe* policy.

Quite clearly there was considerable popular support for *Roe* and there were also major interest groups such as the National Abortion Rights Action League (NARAL), Planned Parenthood, and the National Organization for Women (NOW) who vigorously championed abortion rights. In other words, while the Court's decision in *Roe* made enemies, it also had many friends. And what has happened ever since 1973 is that the Court's friends and enemies on the abortion issue have fought a political and judicial war over the implementation of the *Roe* policy.

Table 6.2 Public opinion poll data on support for *Roe v. Wade**

Time	% support
February 1974	52
October 1976	60
February 1979	60
September 1985	50
January 1989	56
September 1991	57

*All readings from *Harris* polls except that for 1991, taken from the *Gallup* poll. Both *Harris* and *Gallup* misrepresented the *Roe* decision somewhat by suggesting that abortion was only a constitutional right during the first three months of pregnancy.[5]

Table 6.3 Public support for legal abortion under specific circumstances (%)

Year	Rape	Fetal defect	Mother's health endangered	Can't afford more children	Don't want more children	Any reason
1972	74.1	74.3	83.0	45.6	37.6	n.a.
1973	80.6	82.2	90.6	51.7	46.1	n.a.
1974	82.7	82.6	90.4	52.3	44.6	n.a.
1977	80.5	83.1	88.0	51.6	44.4	36.5
1980	80.2	80.3	87.7	49.6	45.2	39.4
1985	78.0	76.1	86.8	42.4	39.1	35.7
1988	76.7	76.2	85.6	40.4	38.8	34.6
1991	82.3	79.4	88.0	46.1	42.7	40.8

Source: L. Epstein, J. Segal, H. Spaeth and T. Walker, *The Supreme Court Compendium: Data, Decisions and Developments*. Washington, DC, 1994 p. 599.

Pro-life politicians at the national level made literally hundreds of attempts squarely to overturn *Roe* by constitutional amendment or statute. These frontal assaults all failed by some margin, however, simply because they were too drastic to command majority support. But national politicians achieved a notable success with an indirect attack on *Roe* when the Hyde Amendment was passed in 1976 and in every subsequent year. The Hyde Amendment withdrew Medicaid funds for virtually all abortions, meaning that poor women who depended on the programme for their health care would now have to pay for their own abortions. Thus in its first full year of operation, the Hyde Amendment cut Medicaid abortions in 1978 to 2,000 compared with 295,000 in 1977.⁶

For many members of Congress, the Hyde Amendment seemed to be a useful point of compromise. It avoided a direct attack both on the Court and the *Roe* abortion right, but also gave some satisfaction to anti-*Roe* citizens by ensuring that their tax dollars would not be used to pay for what they opposed. The main losers, of course, were poor Medicaid recipients: the Hyde Amendment was intended to make it difficult, if not impossible, for them to have abortions.

Unsurprisingly, the Hyde Amendment was challenged in the Courts as a violation of the constitutional abortion rights of Medicaid recipients. But in what many saw as a tactical retreat by the Justices, the Court ruled 5 to 4 in *Harris v. McRae* (1980) that the Hyde Amendment was a legitimate exercise of the spending power of Congress. The *Roe* abortion right was thus refined to mean that while everyone had a right to choose an abortion, very few had the right to have it paid for by the government, even if all their other medical care was covered by Medicaid.

Presidents Reagan and Bush took the logic of the Hyde Amendment further by stopping federal funding for any kind of government programme that assisted abortion. Thus, in 1988, Reagan introduced the so-called 'gag rule' forbidding any federally-funded family planning programme from even discussing abortion with clients. The Supreme Court upheld this action in *Rust v. Sullivan* (1991).

President Reagan also made a determined effort to ensure that only those opposed to *Roe v. Wade* would be nominated to the federal courts, especially the Supreme Court. Of his three appointees, Justice Scalia has been a resolute opponent of *Roe*, but Justices O'Connor and Kennedy have been less radical.

Despite these major initiatives in Washington, most of the anti-*Roe* campaign has been conducted at the state level. In fact States and local units of government led the way in eliminating funds and facilities for abortions. They also exploited the powers of regulation left to them by *Roe* to try to restrict women's freedom of choice in other ways. Thus the State of Missouri enacted legislation requiring a woman to gain her husband's consent to an abortion, while the city of Akron, Ohio, required women seeking abortions to be read 'information' about abortions that was thinly-disguised anti-abortion propaganda.

Yet a further strand to the pro-life campaign has been direct action by the more militant activists. Operation Rescue, for example, seeks to

prevent women from entering clinics to have abortions, either by phys-
ically blocking access to them or by pressuring women not to enter
them.

All of these anti-*Roe* tactics have ended up back in the federal courts
for rulings on their constitutionality. The Supreme Court has struck
some down, including those requiring a husband's consent (*Planned
Parenthood v. Danforth*, 1976); upheld others, including those eliminating all traces of material government support for abortions (*Webster
v. Reproductive Health Services*, 1989); and drawn up guidelines for
others, including clinic protest activity (*Madsen v. Women's Health
Centre*, 1994).

Two major questions arise from this. First, was the Supreme Court
forced by the opponents of *Roe* to capitulate or retreat? Second, was
the Court's actual abortion policy seriously undermined?

The answer to the first is that the Court has made significant concessions to anti-*Roe* sentiment and, at one point, came within a whisker
of actually abandoning *Roe*. When *Roe* was first decided, there was no
hint that the Court intended the States' residual regulatory powers
over abortion policy to be used to thwart the exercise of abortion
rights. Yet by allowing States and the federal government to withdraw
counselling and medical services, to cut off funds and to mandate
informed consent and waiting-period procedures, the Court has effectively narrowed the scope and exercise of abortion rights.

In doctrinal terms, the Court has shifted from the Roe stipulation
that States must demonstrate a 'compelling' reason to interfere with a
woman's abortion right to one where States need only refrain from
imposing an 'undue burden' on that right. Furthermore, in *Webster v.
Reproductive Health Services* (1989) and *Planned Parenthood v. Casey*
(1992), the Court only upheld the basic constitutional right to abortion
by votes of 5 to 4. The initial *Roe* case was decided 7 to 2. This change
in the strength of support for *Roe* on the Court reflects, of course, the
efforts of Presidents Reagan and Bush to appoint anti-*Roe* Justices.

The evidence of the abortion conflict suggests, therefore, that the
Court is certainly vulnerable to concerted attacks by opponents of its
decisions. It can be forced to adjust its constitutional reasoning to
make concessions to its opponents in order to stave off a more damaging attack on its decisions and, indeed, its authority. The Court is
so vulnerable simply because other branches of government possess
powerful means – particularly the control of financial and other
resources – of resisting or circumventing the Court's decisions. And

without at least some support from those branches, the Court is too weak to enforce its will.

On the other hand, the basic constitutional right to an abortion that was announced in *Roe* remains in place. Whereas before *Roe* many States prohibited virtually all abortions, they can now prohibit very few. To have withstood the onslaught by pro-life forces over the last two decades, then, the Court must have resources of its own. The first, and most obvious, is the lifetime tenure of members of the Court. Had the Justices been subjected to re-election, it is hard to believe that many would have survived the conservative mood of the 1980s.

Second, the Court had its defenders. Not only is there considerable public support for abortion under certain circumstances, but pro-choice interest groups and politicians have lined up behind the Court. One notable demonstration of their power occurred when they formed a coalition to defeat the nomination of an arch-enemy of *Roe*, Robert Bork, to the Court in 1987.

The third main factor in the survival of *Roe*, however, is a para-doxical one. Three Justices who seem to believe that *Roe* was wrongly decided found a reason to uphold it in the very political campaign that was waged against it. Justices Sandra Day O'Connor and Anthony Kennedy were appointed by President Reagan, who, as we have seen, made opposition to *Roe* the 'acid test' of selection. Justice Souter was appointed by President Bush, who had also made his opposition to *Roe* very clear. Most observers believed that the three Justices would prob-ably vote to overturn *Roe*, although none had ever said so specifically. Together with the guaranteed votes against *Roe* of Chief Justice Rehn-quist and Justices White, Scalia and Thomas, the end of the constitu-tional right to abortion seemed certain when the Court heard *Planned Parenthood v. Casey* (1992).

Justices O'Connor, Kennedy and Souter, however, decided to uphold the basis of the right to abortion, not because they believed it was justified by the Constitution, but because it had become an impor-tant legal and social reality since 1973. It therefore deserved great respect both as a legal precedent and as a right to which people had become accustomed. The three Justices emphasised that the Supreme Court was a *court* dedicated to *law*. It should not, therefore, behave like a legislature and change its decisions with every change in per-sonnel. People were entitled to stability and predictability in the law, even where an original decision may have been wrongly decided.

Unless the Supreme Court placed great value on stability, it risked losing its special authority in the American system of government. If the people became convinced that the Court would change its decisions with every change in the political climate or with every new appointment, then it would be perceived as just another political body with no special claim to interpret the Constitution. Above all, said the three Justices, the Court must not retreat 'under political fire' of the kind brought to bear by the pro-life movement since 1973 (see also Chapter Four).

The *Casey* opinion of O'Connor, Kennedy and Souter is clear evidence that they had seen grave dangers resulting from the activist policy-making role adopted by the Court over recent decades. First came the liberal activism and then the conservative backlash. The result was that the Court was looking increasingly less like an autonomous judicial body above politics and more like a political football being kicked around by contending social activists. Both the law and the Court itself were being dragged too far into the political mire.

The three Justices sought, therefore, to pull back. This they did first by upholding the essence of *Roe* and thereby asserting the primacy of legal and judicial values. But secondly, they allowed States greater powers to regulate abortion under the new 'undue burden' standard and thereby returned the details of abortion policy back to the States and their political arenas for resolution. It was an astute compromise, showing that tactical and strategic calculations are also part of the Court's decision-making process.

Abortion policy

We have seen that when subjected to constant attack for over twenty years, the Court was forced into a partial retreat over the constitutional right to an abortion. But what about the impact of its decisions on women's lives? Does the abortion rights episode indicate that the Court is a powerful body, able to instigate dramatic change in social reality?

Before answering this question, it is worth noting that there have been two basic schools of thought on this. As Gerald Rosenberg's major study of the Court and social reform reminds us, there are the rival concepts of the 'dynamic court' and the 'constrained court'.[7]

The dynamic court emphasises the Supreme Court's freedom from electoral constraints. The Justices are not bound by majority opinion and minorities and other disadvantaged groups can gain access to them on a more or less equal basis with those with far greater political power. Moreover, the Court has flexibility of action, unlike legislative and bureaucratic bodies who are often locked into the defence of vested interests. It also argued that the Court can have an important role as a catalyst for others, reminding them of their rights and duties under the Constitution. Thus the dynamic court can inspire social change, both directly and indirectly.

The constrained court, by contrast, is a weak body. It deals with constitutional rights, but the actual exercise of rights is often dependent upon possession of resources. Thus there may be a right to own a Rolls-Royce, but that right is meaningless for the many without the means to buy one. The question of resources also has implications for compliance with Court decisions, since it highlights the dependence of the judiciary on the elected branches of government to enforce its policies. At best, then, the Court can declare the existence of theoretical rights, but these will only be made meaningful if elected politicians are in agreement with them and if they give them a high priority. The constrained court is thus limited in the scope of the issues it can address and is wholly dependent on others for any impact. It is not, therefore, an independent instigator of major social change.

Rosenberg applied the concepts of dynamic court and constrained court to the Supreme Court's decisions on, amongst other issues, abortion. He found that the evidence of impact tends to support the concept of the constrained court.

In the first place, he notes that the number of abortions performed each year began to rise rapidly three years *before* the *Roe* decision. And that *Roe* did not increase the rate at which that rise continued throughout the 1970s.[8]

This failure by *Roe* to make a difference in the already upward trend suggests that, rather than initiate a revolution, 'the Supreme Court merely acknowledged one in progress and let it continue'.[9] As Rosenberg concedes, however, the Court may have added a dynamic element. For abortions before *Roe* were carried out largely in States which had liberalised their abortion statutes. There is no guarantee that many more States would have joined the trend without *Roe* requiring them to do so. The Court may therefore have helped to spread the abortion revolution already underway.

A second source of evidence about the power of the Court to initiate reform are the figures on abortion provision. In theory, *Roe* nationalised the right to abortion in the sense that all American women were free to exercise it, regardless of the State or locality in which they lived. In practice, however, State and locality *do* matter. For many States have made it very difficult for a woman to obtain an abortion by forbidding the use of public funds and other resources, and by imposing regulations designed to discourage and impede women who seek abortions (see Table 6.4). The net result is that the *Roe* decision has had a varied impact upon the States.

Table 6.4 States banning/providing use of public funds for abortions, 1991–92

Banning		Providing
Alabama	Arizona	Alaska
Arkansas	Colorado	California
Delaware	Florida	Connecticut
Georgia	Illinois	Hawaii
Indiana	Kansas	Maryland
Kentucky	Louisiana	New Jersey
Maine	Massachusetts	New York
Minnesota	Mississippi	North Carolina
Missouri	Montana	Oregon
Nevada	New Hampshire	Vermont
New Mexico	North Dakota	Washington
Ohio	Oklahoma	West Virginia
Rhode Island	South Carolina	(12)*
South Dakota	Tennessee	
Texas	Utah	
	(30)*	

* The position in other States is unclear.

Source: B. Craig and D. O'Brien, *Abortion and American Politics*, Chatham, N.J., 1993, adapted from Table 10.1, pp. 351–3.

Of course, most women in the United States do not rely on public funds for their health care and hence their abortions. As a consequence, only the poor are affected by state policies cutting off public funds. All women, however, are affected by the number of hospitals and clinics willing to perform abortions in their State. And either because of state law or other forms of resistance to *Roe*, the number of such facilities varies widely from State to State, as Table 6.5 indicates.

Although geographical area and population size complicate comparisons, it is clear that women have a much harder time obtaining abortions in some States than in others. Missouri and Washington, for example, are of roughly similar size and population: yet Washington has more than three times the number of providers than Missouri and around 60 per cent more abortions.

However, it is also true that a strongly anti-abortion State like Pennsylvania still has 90 providers and over 50,000 abortions a year. This demonstrates the limits of the States' ability to resist *Roe*, when private clinics are willing to perform abortions. And in Texas, the State involved in the *Roe* decision, there are some 100,000 abortions a year, the vast majority of which would have been illegal without the Court's decision.

Table 6.5 Number of abortion providers and number of abortions performed, selected states, 1991–92

State	Abortion providers	Abortions
California*	608	311,720
Hawaii*	53	11,170
Kentucky	9	11,520
Louisiana	13	17,340
Missouri	20	19,490
New York*	305	183,980
Pennsylvania	90	51,830
South Dakota	1	900
Texas	91	100,690
Washington*	68	31,220

*States in italics have liberal abortion policies; the others are amongst the most restrictive.

Source: B. Craig and D. O'Brien, *Abortion and American Politics*, Chatham, N.J., 1993, adapted from Table 10.1, pp. 351–3.

In short, while Rosenberg is right in stressing that the Court did not initiate the liberalising trend, it did give it a further push. This suggests that the Court cannot be an autonomous agent of social change, but it can play a supporting role. In the final chapter, we will discuss further this and other political and legal roles played by the Supreme Court.

Summary

While the Court can depend on a good deal of respect and deference, it also encounters considerable resistance to its decisions when it provokes the elected branches of government, interest groups or public opinion. Other branches of government have a variety of formal and informal means of resisting the Court. Whether or not the Court is forced to retreat on these occasions depends in part upon the extent to which its allies rally to its defence. More important in the long term, however, is whether new appointees to the Court have been selected for the express purpose of overturning unpopular decisions. Either way, however, the power of the Supreme Court is constrained by the Justices' knowledge that too many provocative decisions will undermine its legitimacy, as well as its power. The likelihood of significant resistance is thus something the Court may have to consider as it ponders a major decision.

Notes

1 L. Fisher, *Constitutional Dialogues: Interpretation As Political Process*, Princeton, 1988.
2 *Ibid.*, p. 225.
3 B. Woodward and S. Armstrong, *The Brethren*, New York, 1979, p. 219.
4 K. Luker, *Abortion and the Rights of Motherhood*, London, 1984, p. 138.
5 L. Epstein, J. Segal, L. Spaeth and T. Walker, *The Supreme Court Compendium: Data, Decisions and Developments*, Washintgon, D.C., 1994, p. 600. The *Harris* poll question was 'In 1973, the US Supreme Court decided that state laws which made it a crime to have an abortion up to three months of pregnancy were unconstitutional, and that the decision of whether or not to have an abortion should be left to the woman and her doctor to decide. In general, do you oppose or favour the US Supreme Court decision making abortion up to three months of pregnancy legal?'.
6 K. Petersen, 'The Public Funding of Abortion Services', *International and Comparative Law Quarterly*, XXXIII, 1984, pp. 158–80, particularly p. 170.
7 Rosenberg, *The Hollow Hope. Can Courts Bring About Social Change?*, Chicago, 1988, Chapter 1.
8 *Ibid.*, p. 179.
9 *Ibid.*

Seven—The role of the Supreme Court in American government and politics

In the previous chapters, we have analysed different aspects of the Supreme Court's structures and processes. We have noted its political and legal dimensions, its powers and limitations and the controversies it has generated at different moments in its history. In this final chapter, we bring all these elements together and ask the ultimate question, 'What is the role of the Supreme Court in American government and politics?'

All government and politics is about power. And since the United States Supreme Court is a co-equal branch of the federal government, it too is about power. Over fifty years ago, one of the most astute observers of the Court, Robert H. Jackson, wrote:

> Nearly every significant decision of the Supreme Court has to do with power – power of government, power of officials - and hence it is always concerned with the social and economic interests involved in the allocation, denial, or recognition of power.[1]

The Supreme Court and the allocation of power

The most basic role of the Supreme Court as the authoritative interpreter of the Constitution is to allocate power. The Court does this in two broad ways. First, it allocates power between different branches of government, usually when those branches are in dispute over who has control of public policy. The dispute may be between the federal government and a State; or it may be between different branches of the federal government, say, the presidency and the Congress.

Secondly, the Supreme Court allocates power between government and citizens. All governmental laws and regulations affect some interests within American society, whether they be the interests of individuals or of organisations such as corporations, professional associations or pressure groups. And while many of those affected may see benefits in the particular government action in question, other will perceive themselves as harmed. This 'disadvantaged' interest may urge politicians to change government policy, to alter the distribution of benefits within the policy. Alternatively, however, they may assert that government lacks the power to make the policy altogether, and that complaint is addressed to the Supreme Court.

The Supreme Court's role in allocating power between different branches of government and between government and citizenry derives directly from its duty to uphold the Constitution. For it is the Constitution which allocates power within the American political system. Since the Constitution is not self-enforcing, however, the Supreme Court acts as the instrument and mouthpiece of constitutional enforcement. Or to recall Chief Justice Hughes' famous aphorism: 'We are under a Constitution, but the Constitution is what the Supreme Court says it is.'

Of course, as we have seen, the Supreme Court is not the only governmental or political body which attempts to allocate power, but it is unique in that it possesses the ultimate authority or legitimacy to do so. Others may therefore assert power, but only the Supreme Court can confer (or withhold) legitimacy upon that assertion, because it alone speaks with the authority of the Constitution. To put it another way, only the Supreme Court can *constitutionalise* allocations of powers and rights.

The Supreme Court's allocation of power as political prize

However, as we have repeatedly seen, the Supreme Court does not operate in a political vacuum and its role as the authoritative allocator of powers and rights is no exception. Indeed, precisely because the Court can bestow the ultimate political prize of constitutional approval and legitimacy, its blessing is seen as a valuable resource to be won by contending social groups and political institutions. In this sense, the Supreme Court becomes not merely the site of political conflict, but the very object of that conflict.

The Supreme Court's power to confer constitutional legitimacy must be seen, then, as an important political resource to be fought for and won by opposing interests and organisations in American society. For while Congress and the President can bestow favours through legislation, those gains may be undone by defeat at the next election. Once the Supreme Court has *constitutionalised* an allocation of power or rights, however, a new Congress or President will need supermajoritarian support to overthrow the Court's decision through constitutional amendment. In short, the Supreme Court's constitutional blessing is the ultimate prize in American politics.

Who benefits from the Supreme Court's allocation of power?

Because constitutional legitimacy bestowed by the Supreme Court is of prime importance, analysts have tried to discover whether there is, over time, any broad pattern to the way in which the Court allocates power. Does it, for example, tend to favour some social groups over others, or one branch of government over another?

Certainly for much of its history, the Court has favoured what may loosely be termed the vested interests of business and capital. This is hardly surprising, given the strong emphasis on property rights in American political and constitutional history. Since the 1930s, however, as we saw in Chapter One, this emphasis has given way to a focus on the civil rights and liberties of individuals and certain disadvantaged groups.

This has led many observers to argue that the Supreme Court has changed its fundamental role, from being a bastion of the rich and powerful to being the champion of disadvantaged individuals and minorities. This, in turn, may suggest that the Supreme Court is a free-floating institution that may transform its political role as and when it sees fit.

At first glance, this concept of the Court's role may seem attractive. And, indeed, as we shall see below, it is not without merit. However, if we examine the Court's historical role at the broadest level, and take into account the political environment in which it must operate, it becomes clear that the judicary's freedom of manoeuvre is quite constrained.

The Supreme Court and the national majority

Some decades ago, Robert Dahl wrote what is still today one of the most convincing analyses of the Court's broad role.[2] Dahl's central argument was that the Supreme Court has an inevitable tendency to favour the most powerful groups in society, or, more precisely, the national law-making majority at any given moment. He wrote:

> [T]he policy views dominant on the Court are never for long out of line with the policy views dominant among the law-making majorities of the

United States. Consequently it would be most unrealistic to suppose that the Court would, for more than a few years at most, stand against any major alternatives sought by the law-making majority.[3]

Dahl rested his thesis on both history and logic. First then, it is important to note that the Court only rarely declares federal laws unconstitutional – just 133 in whole or in part up to 1990. On the other hand, it quite frequently invalidates state and local legislation. Thus for every federal law it has declared unconstitutional, the Court has struck down about nine non-national enactments.[4] This suggests very clearly that the Court is far more willing to override the policy preferences of local law-makers than the national law-making majority.

Secondly, Dahl points out that Justices of the Supreme Court are appointed by the national law-making majority and that a new Justice is appointed, on average, about every two years.[5] This means that when a national law-making coalition is able to hold office over a reasonable period of time, it is likely to be able to place a majority of sympathetic Justices on the Court.

Third, as we saw in Chapter Six, there are many pressures that elected politicians can bring to bear upon the Court, even when the Justices are not especially sympathetic to their political goals. Over time, then, the Court can be forced to retreat, if not to capitulate completely.

Dahl concludes from these arguments that majorities usually get their way eventually and the Supreme Court will join the dominant national political coalition of law-makers. Hence, he says: 'The main task of the Court is to confer legitimacy on the fundamental policies of the successful coalition.'[6] Viewed from this perspective, the Supreme Court of the United States plays the role of reassuring the country that the policies of the national law-making majority are compatible with the Constitution and therefore worthy of respect and observance. The most important role of the Court, then, is to legitimate (or de-legitimate) political continuity and change.

The Supreme Court and symbolic power

It is clear that this is, in many respects, a symbolic role performed by the Court. This is not surprising in a country where constitutionalism has been raised to the level of a secular religion. And if the American people worship the Constitution, then the Supreme Court sits at the apex of the church hierarchy. The mystique of the Constitution and the rituals of the judicial process combine to lend an air of almost divine authority to the Court's decisions: unfathomable, perhaps, but nonetheless reassuring. And so just as in the United Kingdom the Archbishop of Canterbury legitimates the new Queen by placing the Crown upon her head, so the Supreme Court legitimates a new political majority by conferring the blessing of the Constitution upon it.

This symbolic power is considerable but also fragile. On the one hand, it can be sufficiently compelling to command obedience or acquiescence from both citizens and political elites. Thus President Eisenhower felt obliged to send troops to Little Rock, Arkansas, in 1957, in order to desegregate the local high school. He did so even though he earnestly believed that the Supreme Court's decision in *Brown v. Board of Education* had been wrong. On the other hand, the Court's symbolic power rests in no small measure upon the notion that the Justices are 'above politics'. Therefore the more embroiled they become in the messy politics of national policy-making, the more likely they are to lose their exalted aura. To an extent this is precisely what has happened over the last thirty years or so.

As we saw in Chapter One, the federal judiciary has played an increasingly important role in setting national policy on controversial matters such as abortion and capital punishment. The problem for the Court was not merely that it took some daring initiatives on these issues, but that the Justices quickly became perceived as mere partisans in an essentially political conflict and hence not much different from ordinary politicians. That in turn persuaded ideologically-motivated politicians and interest groups to treat the Court as if it were merely just another political body, whose membership could be bullied and manipulated for basic partisan purposes.

By the late 1980s, the Court appeared to be on a downward spiral into full-scale politicisation and thus in danger of losing its precious mystique. In recent years, however, some of the Justices have made a concerted effort to draw back from the abyss. As we saw in Chapter Four, Justices O'Connor, Kennedy and Souter took the opportunity provided by the challenge to abortion rights in *Planned Parenthood v. Casey* (1992) to argue that the Supreme Court must not be seen to alter its interpretation of the Constitution every time a new Justice is appointed.

Above all, said the three Justices, meaningful constitutionalism required the Supreme Court to do more than pay lip-service to judicial and legal values of continuity and enduring principle: it must be seen to give them priority over political expediency. If not, then the Supreme Court will lose its distinctive claim on the loyalty of the American people.

Updating the Constitution

As long as the Supreme Court retains its role as the prime legitimator of political change in the United States, it will effectively be responsible for updating the Constitution. Although this is sometimes derided as the 'unjudicial' task of 'keeping the Constitution in tune with the times', it is in fact a serious and important role. In theory, the Constitution may be amended to take account of political and social change through the provisions of Article V. These provisions, however, are so unwieldy and time-consuming that they can only be infrequently implemented.

Moreover, because constitutional amendments require the approval of three-fifths of the members of both houses of Congress and three-quarters of the legislatures of the fifty States, the amendment process can easily be blocked by quite small minorities. It is little wonder, then, that there have been only twenty-six amendments to the Constitution since 1789.

During the same period, however, American society has fundamentally changed and its political, economic and social needs along with it. In particular, the role of government has changed with the acquisition of vast new responsibilities undreamt of by those who wrote the Constitution in the eighteenth century. The Constitution, therefore, must be flexible to meet changing times and needs. And if the process of constitutional amendment is too cumbersome and unresponsive to accommodate these changes, then the Court can breathe flexibility into the Constitution through 'interpretation' of its clauses.

Very often, such judicial amendment of the Constitution has had little or nothing to do with genuine interpretation and everything to do with responding to political demands for change. Thus, in order to allow the federal government to take over responsibility from the States for almost anything it wishes, the Court has interpreted the federal commerce power so broadly as to render it almost meaningless (see Chapter One).[7]

Nevertheless, as a pragmatic response to changing times and values, constitutional amendment in the guise of constitutional interpretation by the Supreme Court performs a valuable service to American government. And as long as the Court plays this role with restraint, by responding to majoritarian demands rather than initiating radical new political arrangements, it will continue to enjoy tacit approval in most quarters. For the simple fact is, there is no better way of dealing with the contradictory demands of an enduring and stable constitution on the one hand and the need for change and flexibility on the other.

The Supreme Court as policy-maker

The roles of legitimator of political change and moderniser of the Constitution involve the most elevated functions of the Supreme Court. At a more down-to-earth level, however, the Court can play an important role in making national policy.

Even Dahl, who stressed the essentially weak and passive nature of the Court's power, acknowledged that the Court is also a policy-maker in its own right. And in the years since he first outlined his thesis, events have only reinforced the notion of the Court as a national policy-maker.

Dahl wrote at a time when American politics was characterised by a broad consensus. Moreover, from the 1890s to the 1960s, there was a marked tendency for either the Democrats or the Republicans to form a majority coalition which controlled national law-making. Under these circumstances, it was clearly difficult for the Court to go out on a political limb and to defy Congress and the President. When it did so, in its struggle with the Roosevelt administration over the New Deal, the Court was eventually forced into an ignominious retreat.

Since the late 1960s, however, the United States has experienced an electoral de-alignment in which no party seems capable of building a majority coalition across the board. The result has often been 'divided government', with one party controlling the presidency and the other party controlling one or both houses of Congress. Furthermore, this dealignment is based upon a loss of consensus among the public at large on many issues, including those which centrally involve civil liberties and rights. These, of course, are the very issues which lay at the heart of the Court's contemporary agenda.

The Supreme Court is thus confronted with a divided society and a divided political elite. And since it is not constrained by a law-making or public majority on many issues, it has greater scope for the independent use of its own powers. Thus, as we saw in Chapter One, the Supreme Court has been able to use its powers of constitutional and statutory interpretation to influence or even initiate policies to an unprecedented degree. Of course, the power of interpretation inherently entails policy-making power. But the more unconstrained the Court is by its political environment, the greater is the scope for judicial policy-making.

It should be noted immediately that other political actors, such as Congress and the President, do not necessarily object to judicial policy-making. For example, Congress sometimes deliberately leaves legislation vague, either because it is not sure what it wants or because its members could not agree on certain issues. On these occasions, Congress hopes that the Court will supply the detail for legislation, safe in the knowledge that it can always rewrite what it finds objectionable.

Such policy-making in the guise of statutory interpretation is nothing new in American politics. As Walter Murphy pointed out, what is probably the outstanding example dates back to 1890, when Congress passed the Sherman Antitrust Act. Congress was responding to increasing public pressures to prevent monopolies, or 'trusts', from achieving a stranglehold on various sectors of the economy. But in the legislation that was eventually passed after considerable debate, Congress gave no definition of what these terms meant nor criteria for identifying them when they existed. And the eponymous Senator Sherman openly stated that he was leaving it to the courts to fill the details.[8]

Even when constitutional interpretation is involved, politicians may still welcome Supreme Court policy-making on controversial issues. After all, many elected politicians prefer to avoid making controversial decisions themselves, since they fear antagonising voters. Far better to allow the Justices of the Supreme Court to take the heat, while the politicians explain to their constituents that they are powerless to act in the face of a constitutional ruling.

Most of all, of course, elected politicians are grateful for judicial policy-making when they agree with its outcomes. Conversely, they are most likely to attack the Court, and rail about improper judicial intervention in legislative matters, when they strongly disagree with its outcomes. And the same is largely true of interest groups and the general public. The simple fact is that many if not most people outside of the Court's legal audience, and not a small number within it, are moved by the results of judicial policy-making rather than its methods.

The question then is not whether the Supreme Court makes policy, but how often, how decisively and with what results. Interpretation calls policy-making functions into play, but these are constrained by the political environment and the Justices themselves. Members of the Supreme Court are acutely aware that they do not make decisions in a political vacuum and that they must take into account the likely reactions of other political actors.

This interactive concept of judicial policy-making was captured in Louis Fisher's notion of 'constitutional dialogues'.[9] Most Supreme Court decisions contribute something to policy-making, but those decisions do not stand alone. Neither do they necessarily constitute the 'final word' on policy. Other political bodies react to them (or not) and thus a 'dialogue' occurs between the Court and those bodies. That dialogue may be angry, cooperative or compliant. The Court may be faced with a series of legal cases which challenge its ruling or assaults on it from the political arena. And as we saw with the history of the abortion issue, the Court may be forced to retreat to accommodate political hostility to its rulings. Nevertheless, whatever the policy which eventually emerges from a 'constitutional dialogue', it is likely to be one which bears at least some imprint of the federal judiciary.

For all the criticisms levelled against judicial policy-making in recent years, many of them justified, it should not be forgotten that the Supreme Court can bring valuable and distinctive perspectives to bear on public policy. Most importantly, it can remind politicians and the public of the long-term values of the nation which are enshrined in the Constitution, but which may be forgotten in the rush for short-term political gain and quick solutions. And where the Constitution is clear, a determined judiciary can hold the line for a while against intemperate legislative majorities. The Court must never forget, however, that if it goes too far, too fast in its policy-making role, it is likely to meet with a sustained and damaging counter-attack.

There is thus a good deal of ambivalence about the Supreme Court's policy-making role. On the one hand, politicians, interest groups and the general public have an attachment to the mythic view of the Court as a non-partisan oracle, which rises above politics to tell the nation what the Founding Fathers would have thought or decided. On the other hand, the same politicians know that the Court must play some policy-making role and are glad that it should do so when the results are unobjectionable.

For their part, the Justices of the Supreme Court know that they must cultivate the mythic view at least to some extent, even as they attempt to resolve some of the most difficult and divisive political conflicts. Supreme Court policy-making, therefore, is an art which demands both political sensitivity and regard for constitutional values which transcend immediate political concerns. Where the balance lies between the two varies with the issue and the wider political environment.

When the Court gets the balance right, it can make significant, even innovative contributions to policy and be praised for doing so. The prime example is the Warren Court of the 1950s and the initiatives it took to end racial segregation. When it gets it wrong, however, the Court will be the target of outraged allegations of usurping the prerogatives of the people's elected representatives and undermining democracy itself. The Court's decisions against the New Deal in the 1930s and those in the 1970s on abortion serve to illustrate the wrath that the Justices can bring down on themselves. When it comes to policy-making, then, the Supreme Court must keep one eye on the Constitution and the other on the political climate.

The Court, conflict resolution and political stability

Implicit in all the roles played by the Court is the duty to resolve political and social conflicts. Although the Court performs this role by settling legal disputes, it has long been understood that, in the United States, political conflicts are frequently transformed into legal cases.

Indeed, so routine has become the judicial resolution of essentially political disputes in the United States that it barely causes comment outside of legal circles. This familiarity, however, should not blind us to the profound importance of this role in the American political system. For the ultimate purpose of this conflict resolution is not to decide whether Party X is entitled to Legal Claim Y, but rather to preserve the stability of the political system itself. As Henry Stumpf pointed out, all courts serve the needs of the regime that created them and they do this by resolving disputes which are potentially disruptive to the political order:

> Put simply, disputes threaten social stability, and one function of government is to maintain that stability ... Disputes are a cancerous growth on the body politic; they must be dealt with in the interest of the very survival of the regime.[10]

Why should courts perform this function of resolving disputes? Primarily, because courts are often seen, rightly or wrongly, as being more impartial than political bodies and thus in a better position to arrive at a just resolution to a dispute. In considering the role of the

United States Supreme Court in this respect, we must also remember that it is acknowledged as the authoritative interpreter of the Constitution. This means that the Supreme Court benefits not only from the general attribute of courts as relatively impartial, but also from the specific claim that its judgments are rooted in the Nation's ideals. In short, most parties to disputes resolved by the Court accept that they have had a fair hearing on their claim.

Such a sense of justice done and justice seen to be done benefits the regime with regard to both winners and losers. Most obviously, losers tend to accept their legal and constitutional defeat, even if they continue to believe that they are morally in the right. Their sense of grievance may live on, but they lack the conviction to perpetuate the conflict.

A more subtle and complex situation may surround those who win important or new rights in the Supreme Court. Their sense of grievance is diminished because their claim has been vindicated. Yet even where this victory entails a defeat for the status quo previously championed by the regime, the actual costs to the regime may turn out to be far less than imagined.

Courts, it must be remembered, *declare* rights but are forced to rely on other branches of government to *enforce* or *deliver* them. And as we saw in Chapter Six, the political branches of government in the United States can be adept at resisting or refusing compliance with Supreme Court decisions. The net result may be that the winners in a Supreme Court case involving substantial policy change may have gained only a symbolic or partial victory. To use a sporting metaphor, the regime declares a winner and presents the trophy, but then refuses to hand over the accompanying cheque.

Some believe that this is more or less what has happened with the campaign for racial equality in the United States. African-Americans won a series of constitutional cases before the Supreme Court in the 1950s and 1960s, which declared them to be equal citizens. This gave them a stake in the system which was previously lacking and reduced the likelihood of a widespread and fundamental challenge to the regime. At the same time, while the legal status of African-Americans was undoubtedly enhanced, their economic and social position within the system improved only marginally. Thus, it can be argued, African-Americans were lulled into acquiescing to a system which offered them only a token of equality, rather than its substance.

Many, of course, dispute this theory and argue that the courts can produce real victories for those oppressed by a majoritarian political process. But whichever view comes closest to the truth, both imply an important role for the Supreme Court in promoting political stability. By acting to defuse regime-threatening conflicts, the Supreme Court can resolve, or at least contain, disputes that the political branches cannot or will not settle.

The Supreme Court as guarantor of civil liberties

For most Americans, however, probably the most valued role performed by the Supreme Court is that of defender of civil liberties against majoritarian or governmental power. American political culture places a high value upon individual liberty and freedom from governmental interference. And in as much as the Supreme Court is identified as the last line of defence against oppressive officialdom and abuse of power, it is held to be an indispensable feature of the American political system.

There are numerous celebrated cases in which the Court has played this role. Perhaps most famous of all is *US v. Nixon* (1974), in which a unanimous Supreme Court ordered President Richard Nixon to release secretly-recorded tapes of White House conversations about the Watergate scandal. Nixon, who had claimed 'executive privilege' to withhold certain tapes, felt bound to comply with the Court's decision. The tapes revealed that Nixon had ordered his staff to cover up the links between the White House and the Watergate burglary and he was forced to resign his office.

Another example of the Court's role in combating governmental abuse of power occurred in 1971, in the so-called *Pentagon Papers* case (*New York Times v. US*). The Pentagon Papers were a secret Defence Department history of US policy-making on the Vietnam War. They revealed that the government had used secrecy to deceive the country about the aims and extent of US involvement in Vietnam. They were leaked to the *New York Times*, which duly published a first instalment. At that point, the Nixon administration tried to prevent any further publication. A 6–3 majority of the Justices, however, ruled that the First Amendment's guarantee of freedom of the press outweighed any government interest in suppressing publication.

These cases cast the Supreme Court in a heroic role for most Americans. And along with the many decisions of the last fifty years upholding the rights of individuals and minorities against repressive governmental action, they have earned the Court a reputation as the champion of freedom and liberty within the American political system.

This does not mean that in every case in which the Court upholds individual freedom, it benefits from strong public support. Indeed, some decisions upholding the rights of communists, religious minorities and criminals, for example, have been highly unpopular. However, at a general level, the Court is highly esteemed as a guarantor of citizens' rights. An interesting example of this occurred in 1987, during the struggle over the nomination of Robert Bork to the Supreme Court. Bork advocated a very narrow concept of constitutional liberties, in which rights were confined to those explicitly mentioned in the Constitution. As such, he was a fierce critic of the Court's creation of a constitutional right to privacy in 1965. That right subsequently proved highly controversial when it was argued, for example, that it protected the right of women to have abortions and the right of gays to have sexual relations. Yet when opponents of Bork's nomination conducted detailed public opinion research, they discovered enormous disquiet over his belief that the Court had exceeded its power in declaring a right to privacy. Quite simply, most Americans thought they should enjoy a right to privacy and were glad that the Court had discovered one in the Constitution.[11]

In short, although Americans disagree over whether rights and liberties deserve protection from government in particular instances, there is a strong consensus behind the idea that the Supreme Court should play a leading role in preserving and even expanding citizens' freedoms.

The indispensable Supreme Court

Reflecting on these different roles, it is immediately apparent that the Supreme Court has become indispensable to the American system of government. Most obviously, the Court has become indispensable to the practice of constitutionalism. For all the flak the Court has taken over the years because of its sometimes controversial interpretations of the Constitution, it is hard to imagine any other institution doing the job better.

The Constitution requires interpretation and few argue that this vital necessity would be better accomplished by either the Congress or the presidency, or indeed the two working together. In terms of allocating power between different branches of government, who would expect the Congress and the presidency to do anything other than seek to enhance their own power? And in terms of resolving conflicts on a just and impartial basis, how many elected politicians would do as well as the Justices in resisting popular pressure or their own ideology?

This does mean that the Court always performs its roles well – far from it. Nor does it mean that there are no disadvantages to having these roles performed by a court of unelected judges. Nevertheless, each negative aspect of the Supreme Court's character is balanced and, I would argue, outweighed by a positive aspect.

To take but the most obvious example. The fact that the Justices are appointed for life has, at times, undermined the just claims of a majority of Americans: the Court in the early years of the New Deal comes readily to mind. On the other hand, the Justices' life tenure frees them from direct public and political pressures and, at the very least, gives the Court the option of defying the illegitimate demands of an unreasonable majority. In short, the Court's role and power involves a trade-off between judicial arbitrariness and judicial independence. And most Americans are prepared to risk the former in order to preserve the latter. That is why, despite all the furore which has at times surrounded the Court, no direct assault on its fundamental power and roles has ever been successful.

But this argument that the Court is the 'least bad' institution to police the Constitution, while important, is an unnecessarily weak and negative defence of its role in contemporary American government. For if we start from the perspective of the framers of the Constitution, the Founding Fathers of American government, the role of the Supreme Court appears in a much more positive light.

The framers did not envisage or design a majoritarian democracy pure and simple, in which the people and their elected representatives reigned supreme. Rather, they created a *constitutional* democracy of *limited* governmental power. Both the Constitution and the limitations embodied within it were built upon enduring principles, including the rights of individuals and checks on majority power. The Supreme Court has played a significant and indispensable role in preserving that vision of good government.

Even when full account is taken of its retrograde actions and the condemnations it has foolishly and deservedly brought upon itself, the Court has eased the tensions between enduring principles and changing social needs by taking a flexible approach to constitutional interpretation. It has earned and retained the respect of Americans in an age of deep cynicism and pessimism about politics. And, particularly in the twentieth century, it has helped preserve and enhance important freedoms at a time of increasing government power and bitter social conflict.

The Supreme Court: a choice of roles

As we noted in Chapter Two, the precise role of the Supreme Court was left unspecified by the framers of the Constitution. It was, therefore, political logic, history and the Justices themselves that determined the roles that the Court would play. In that sense, the role of the Court in American government is not fixed and the Justices have the power to steer it in one direction or another. As we approach the bicentenary of the case which gave the United States judicial review, it is an appropriate moment to ask whether the history of its use suggests that the Supreme Court is better suited to one version of its role rather than another.

For many years now, scholars and politicians have been putting forward their own ideal models for the Supreme Court to follow. For the most part, these models have started from an ideological premise and been designed to achieve particular political goals through judicial action or inaction. As might be expected, contending liberal and conservative theories of the Court have caused a good deal of controversy and generated much heat, if little light. One of the basic flaws of these theories, however, is the implicit assumption that the Court's possibilities are unlimited. Even conservatives write about judicial activism as if it can roam at will through the political terrain of America.

In fact, although the Justices do indeed have some discretion over the precise role of the Court, its field of action is quite narrowly circumscribed by legal and political realities. There is enough scope for choice to allow for different versions of the Court's role, but the range of that choice is not nearly so wide as contending scholars claim. This is essential to bear in mind as we now go on to examine three basic versions of the Court's role and power.

The minimal court

This is currently the version of the Supreme Court preferred by conservatives. They believe the Court should be limited in its role by the interpretive doctrines of originalism/intentionalism and textualism:

that is, the Supreme Court should only act where the framers of the Constitution intended the Court to act or where the plain language of the Constitution suggests the Court should act. The great appeal of this school is that it leaves policy-making to elected politicians, except where the Constitution clearly suggests otherwise. Theoretically, at least, it therefore enhances democracy, while maintaining the basic vision of the Constitution of 1787.

Unfortunately, this version of a minimal court suffers from one fatal weakness: it has been superseded by history. For better or for worse, the Court long ago broke free of its original bounds and has played a creative role in American government and politics. Two major examples suffice to demonstrate this.

In 1937 the Court virtually abandoned its defence of economic liberties in the context of government regulation of business. This was done not so much because the Justices had previously misinterpreted the Constitution on this matter, but because the Great Depression had created enormous political pressures for a change in that interpretation. By acquiescing in a major departure from original intent and judicial precedent, the Court contributed positively to the modernisation of American government and the stability of the social and political system. The lesson of the episode is that the Supreme Court must be free at critical moments to abandon adherence to the letter of the Constitution in order to serve its underlying purposes.

A second example of the weakness of originalism can be found in the issue of unenumerated rights – rights which have no clear foundation in the text of the Constitution. Throughout the twentieth century, the Court has gradually expanded the number of such rights, which now range from the right to marry to the right to have an abortion, and which add up to an unenumerated right to privacy. Although the Court has been bitterly attacked for some of these decisions, the fact is they find general favour with the American public. For as noted earlier, most Americans believe they ought to have a right to privacy even if the Constitution did not give them one. Once again, therefore, the Supreme Court has broken out of the limits imposed by originalism to ensure that the Constitution reflects fundamental developments – progress, if you prefer – in American culture and government.

The minimal vision of the Court breaks down, then, because it ignores much of the history of the interaction of the Court with American politics and society, particularly in the twentieth century. The Court is no less organic an institution than the Congress or the presidency and at least part of the change in its role is due to the demands placed upon it by a rapidly evolving society. Quite simply, we should not expect the Court to stand still and neither should we expect an attempt to turn back the clock to succeed.

The unlimited court

At the opposite end of the spectrum from the minimal court lies the unlimited court. This school of thought is advanced by some contemporary liberals who believe that the Court can and should re-define its own role, free of the original ideas and constraints which inspired its creation. It has been argued, for example, that the Court should abdicate responsibility for settling disputes between Congress and the presidency and between the federal government and the States because, as a practical matter, these can be left to political bargaining and competition between the parties concerned.

On the other hand, the Court should play a much expanded role as a policy-maker on matters of civil rights and liberties, since it is better equipped than any other institution to 'do justice' in this area of government. The most important thing to note about this conception of the Court is that it is no longer bound by the spirit or text of the Constitution when it dispenses justice. It becomes, in essence, a rolling constitutional convention on human rights, empowered to expand the zone of individual liberty wherever it detects an undesirable interference by government in the lives of its citizens.

An unlimited Supreme Court has the great attraction of providing the American people with a wide-ranging and relatively impartial watchdog over governmental policies with significant implications for civil liberties. Unfortunately to allow the Court to exercise such plenary power carries with it a high risk of excessive judicial activism. Once all restraints have been removed from judicial control, what remains of democratic government and the just powers of elected representatives?

This concern is a serious one, as the history of the Court suggests. In periods of general judicial activism, such as the 1920s and 1930s, or the 1960s and 1970s, the Court has found it difficult to draw a line beyond which it will not step. The expansion of judicial power has an internal dynamic all its own, especially as the more the Court does, the more it is asked to do.

A second major count against the unlimited court is that it does not, in fact, have the capacity to make effective policy in many areas of social policy. Lacking the expertise of the other branches of government, as well as control of resources and enforcement mechanisms, the Supreme Court excels at declaring rights rather than delivering them. There is a tragic irony in the fact that the Court's school desegregation decision in *Brown v. Board of Education* inspired so much faith in judicial activism, yet is now increasingly seen as a prime example of the limitations of judicial policy-making. Thus even for those who yearn for an expanded judicial power, they are likely to be disappointed with its results in the long term.

The realistic court

The role of the Supreme Court in American government, therefore, needs to be considered free of nostalgia for a simpler past and free also of inflated expectations. The Court has duties and responsibilities which are crucial in a constitutional democracy and to these it must respond. It cannot, however, rival the mandate and capacities of the elected branches of government and must not therefore attempt too much, too often. What exactly these obligations and constraints demand of the Court will vary over time and political context. But this study suggests that the Court works best when it observes the following guidelines:

First, the Supreme Court is essentially a judicial body with political power. This means that its methods and criteria for decision should be those of the law, not politics. For by retaining its distinctive character as a court of law and by avoiding becoming just another political body, the Court also has its best chance of preserving its authority. The Court is usually at its most vulnerable when its decisions·are perceived as blatantly partisan.

Nevertheless, there is no bright line which separates law from politics. Thus the Court cannot always be indifferent to the political aspects and consequences of its decisions. When the occasion demands, therefore, law may have to give way to politics and the Court must recognise when a particular interpretation of a statute or the Constitution no longer serves the interest of society.

Second, the Supreme Court's power is very limited and can be used effectively to nullify legislative and executive policies only on rare occasions. The fact is that the Court is an interloper in the business of legislation. Neither the Constitution nor democratic theory provides a 'welcome mat' for judicial legislation, but it is tolerated and even applauded on occasion because it can contribute to good government. However, like guests who outstay their welcome, the Court breeds resentment when it is perceived as usurping the prerogatives of the legislative and executive branches. Thus, the Court is wise to husband its resources and expend them on the relatively few occasions when its intervention is clearly justified and likely to prove effective, even in the face of a hostile reaction.

Third, judicial power is essentially negative rather than positive. This means that it is better suited to telling government what *not* to do than it is at telling it what it must *affirmatively* do. Generally speaking, ordering government to cease doing something is relatively clearcut. It is usually obvious when such a decision has been complied with and it also has the great merit of not requiring government to mobilise significant resources in order to achieve compliance. When, on the other hand, the judiciary assigns new, affirmative responsibilities to government, its inherent weaknesses are most likely to be brought into play. The judiciary lacks the experience and expertise on many issues to know exactly how new responsibilities should be fulfilled. And inventing new government duties through individual law suits may distort the broader issues involved. Furthermore, the Supreme Court lacks the control over resources and enforcement mechanisms to oblige government to do something it may never have done before and has no wish to begin doing.

Thus it is relatively easy for the Court to say that States may not discriminate by law against racial minorities. But when the judiciary sets government the goal of positively integrating schools, as opposed to merely ending discriminatory laws, then it engenders a whole host of policy issues which are complex and likely to meet with serious resistance. This has been the Court's experience where it has ordered the busing of children to achieve a certain racial mix in schools and also where it has ordered vast new expenditures by school authorities in order to attract non-minority pupils to predominantly minority schools.

Advocates of an unlimited Supreme Court and other proponents of judicial activism must simply acknowledge that the Supreme Court possesses neither the means nor the authority to rival or supplant legislative and executive action. The conservative Court of the 1930s and the liberal Court of the 1960s have both run into the brick wall of this fundamental fact. In both periods, the Court found that effective judicial solutions to policy problems could not be devised through constitutional interpretation. Moreover, the Court also found that the elected branches of government were not willing to concede ultimate authority over many contemporary issues to the unelected judiciary.

This is not a counsel of despair for the Supreme Court. It is simply to recognise the wisdom of Justice Frankfurter's dictum in *Baker v. Carr* (1962) that:

There is not under our Constitution a judicial remedy for every political mischief. In a democratic society like ours, relief must come through an aroused popular conscience that sears the conscience of the people's representatives.

Advocates of a minimal court, however, also have some realities with which they must come to terms. Above all, they have to live with the fact that judicial review cannot be chained to some unchanging rock called the law. Law, especially constitutional law, is dynamic in that it interacts with an evolving society and the ebb and flow of political conflict. It is simply unavoidable then that the Supreme Court will at times need to escape the confines of the legal past. The Justices, in short, must be allowed discretion, including the discretion to be creative when the political situation demands it. As a result, the kind of predictability, certainty even, about judicial decisions that some of the Court's critics crave is impossible.

Realistically, the Supreme Court never has and never could satisfy the demands of its critics, either on the left or the right. For the former, its power is too limited, while for the latter its objectionable features have become essential elements of American politics.

In practice, therefore, the Supreme Court's role in American government is one characterised by ambiguity as much as by clarity, and by constraint as much as by grandeur. It treads a fine line between law and politics, knowing that it is expected to serve both. It is capable of magnificent declarations of constitutional power and principle, yet frequently retreats behind a judicial cloak in order to avoid controversial pronouncements. All of these characteristics, however, are necessary to the performance of its most important role: to ensure that government in America comports with the demands of the Constitution and that the Constitution comports with the demands of America.

Notes

1 Robert H. Jackson, *The Struggle For Judicial Supremacy*, New York, 1941, p. xii. Jackson was Solicitor General at the time he wrote this book, but was later appointed to the Supreme Court.

2 Robert A. Dahl, 'Decision-Making in a Democracy: The Supreme Court as a National Policy-Maker', *Journal of Public Law*, VI, 1957, pp. 279–95: reprinted in M. Shapiro, *The Supreme Court and Public Policy*, Glenview, Ill., 1969, pp. 57–64. This is not to say that Dahl's article does not have weaknesses: see, for example, Jonathan Casper, 'The Supreme Court and National Policy Making', *American Political Science Review*, LXX, 1976, pp. 50–63.

3 Dahl, 'Decision-Making in a Democracy', p. 61.

4 Between 1789 and 1990, the number of decisions in which the Court struck down federal legislation in whole or in part was 133. The comparable figure for state and local legislation was 1,141. L. Epstein J. Segal, H. Spaeth and T. Walker. *The Supreme Court Compendium: Data, Decisions and Developments*, Washington, D.C., 1994, extrapolated from Tables 2.12 and 2.13, pp. 96–128.

5 Between 1789 and 1996, 108 individuals have served on the Supreme Court.

6 Dahl, 'Decision-Making in a Democracy', p. 64.

7 This process has gone so far that when the Court announced in *US v. Lopez* (1995) that the Commerce clause did not permit Congress to legislate a ban on carrying guns near school premises, the decision was greeted with great surprise. The Commerce clause, it should be remembered, gives Congress the power to regulate commerce between the States. Yet for over fifty years, the Court allowed Congress to use that power to regulate intra-state matters with only the flimsiest connection to commerce between States.

8 W. Murphy, *Elements of Judicial Strategy*, Chicago, 1964, pp. 14–15.

9 L. Fisher, *Constitutional Dialogues: Interpretation as Political Process*, Princeton, N.J., 1988.

10 H. Stumpf, *American Judicial Politics*, San Diego, 1988, p. 455.

11 E. Bronner, *Battle For Justice*, New York, 1989, p. 159.

Guide to further reading

As far as possible, the works listed below are not simply good, but also recent, accessible to Supreme Court beginners and in print. Some, however, have been included simply because they are classics in their particular area.

General reference

Two outstandingly useful volumes have been published in recent years which contain a wealth of factual information about the Supreme Court. Both teachers and students of the Supreme Court will find it invaluable to have ready access to these:

Kermit L. Hall (ed.), *The Oxford Companion to the Supreme Court of the United States*, Oxford, 1992.

L. Epstein, J. Segal, H. Spaeth and T. Walker, *The Supreme Court Compendium: Data, Decisions and Developments*, Washington, D.C., 1994.

Another valuable reference text with a focus on the clauses of the Constitution and their basic interpretation by the Court is:

J. Peltason, *Understanding the Constitution* (11th edn), New York, 1988.

Chapter One—The Court's contemporary agenda

The most detailed and up-to-date work on the process of agenda building on the Court is:

H. Perry, *Deciding to Decide: Agenda Setting in the United States Supreme Court*, Cambridge, Mass., 1991.

Books which bring out the connections between the legal and political contexts of the Court's modern agenda include:

L. Epstein and J. Kobylka, *The Supreme Court and Legal Change: Abortion and the Death Penalty*, Chapel Hill, 1992.

R. McKeever, *Raw Judicial Power? The Supreme Court and American Society* (2nd edn), Manchester (UK), 1995.

R. Pacelle, *The Transformation of the Supreme Court's Agenda: From the New Deal to the Reagan Administration*, Boulder, Col., 1991.

Books which summarise in an accessible fashion a broad range of cases dealt with by the Court include:

H. Abraham and B. Perry, *Freedom and the Court: Civil Rights and Liberties in the United States* (6th edn), New York, 1994

L. Barker and T. Barker, *Civil Liberties and the Constitution: Cases and Commentaries* (7th edn), Englewood Cliffs, N.J., 1994.

Books dealing with specific issues include:

H. Bedau, *The Death Penalty in America* (3rd edn), New York, 1982.

S. Clayton and F. Crosby, *Justice, Gender, and Affirmative Action*, Ann Arbor, 1992.

B. Craig and D. O'Brien, *Abortion and American Politics*, Chatham, N.J., 1993.

G. Curry (ed.), *The Affirmative Action Debate*, Reading, Mass., 1996.

A. Davis and B. Graham, *The Supreme Court, Race, and Civil Rights*, London, 1995.

D. Drakeman, *Church-State Constitutional Issues*, Westport, Conn., 1991.

L. Epstein and J. Kobylka, *The Supreme Court and Legal Change: Abortion and the Death Penalty*, Chapel Hill, 1992.

E. Keynes, *The Court vs. Congress: Prayer, Busing and Abortion*, Durham, N.C., 1989.

A. Kull, *The Color-Blind Constitution*, Cambridge, Mass., 1992.

M. Meltsner, *Cruel and Unusual: The Supreme Court and Capital Punishment*, New York, 1973.

L. Levy, *The Establishment Clause: Religion and the First Amendment*, New York, 1986.

R. Maidment, 'The Supreme Court and Affirmative Action', *Journal of American Studies*, XV, 1981, pp. 341–56.

S. Mezey, *In Pursuit of Equality: Women, Public Policy, and the Federal Courts*, New York, 1992.

R. Mohr, *Gays/Justice: A Study of Ethics, Society and Law*, New York, 1988.

E. Rubin, *Abortion Politics and the Courts: Roe v. Wade and its Aftermath*, New York, 1982.

B. Schwartz, *Behind Bakke: Affirmative Action and the Supreme Court*, New York, 1988.

L. Tribe, *Abortion: The Clash of Absolutes*, New York, 1991.

M. Urofsky, *A Conflict of Rights: The Supreme Court and Affirmative Action*, New York, 1991.

Chapter Two—A historical overview

The best general history of the Supreme Court is:

B. Schwartz, *A History of the Supreme Court*, New York, 1995.

A more interpretive and selective history with a focus on the 'great' Justices and other judges is:

G. White, *The American Judicial Tradition*, Oxford, 1976.

Histories of particular periods in the Court's history include:

V. Blasi (ed.), *The Burger Court: The Counter-Revolution That Wasn't*, New Haven, 1983.

A. Cox, *The Warren Court: Constitutional Decision as an Instrument of Reform*, Oxford, 1968.

D. Savage, *Turning Right: The Making of the Rehnquist Court*, New York, 1992.

J. Simon, *The Centre Holds: The Power Struggle Inside the Rehnquist Court*, New York, 1996.

B. Woodward and S. Armstrong, *The Brethren: Inside the Supreme Court*, New York, 1979.

Chapter Three—Cases, decisions amd judicial procedures

Amongst the books recounting the history of particular cases are:

J. Dreyfuss and C. Lawrence, *The Bakke Case: the Politics of Inequality*, New York, 1979.

M. Faux, *Roe v. Wade*, New York, 1988.

R. Kluger, *Simple Justice: The History of* Brown v. Board of Education, New York, 1976.

A. Lewis, *Gideon's Trumpet*, New York, 1964.

M. Urofsky, *A Conflict of Rights: The Supreme Court and Affirmative Action*, New York, 1991 (on *Johnson v. Transportation Agency*, 1987).

Dealing with the basic details of legal procedures are:

H. Perry, *Deciding to Decide Agenda: Agenda Setting in the United States Supreme Court*, Cambridge, Mass., 1991.

B. Schwartz, *Decision: How the Supreme Court Decides Cases*, New York, 1996.

Also useful on procedures and the broader federal judicial system are:

H. Stumpf, *American Judicial Politics*, San Diego, 1988.

S. Wasby, *The Supreme Court in the Federal Judicial System* (4th edn), Chicago, 1994.

Chapter Four—Politics and judicial review

Many of the works offering either interpretivist or non-interpretivist theories of judicial review are quite challenging for those new to the study of the Supreme Court. Those listed below, therefore, have been selected for their accessibility as well as their importance. For works dealing with extra-judicial influences on the Court, see also the listing for Chapter Six.

S. Barber, *The Constitution of Judicial Power*, Baltimore, 1993.

P. Brest, 'The Misconceived Quest for the Original Understanding', *Boston University Law Review*, LX, 1980, pp. 204–38.

R. Bork, *The Tempting of America: The Political Seduction of the Law*, New York, 1990.

L. Carter, *Contemporary Constitutional Lawmaking: The Supreme Court and the Art of Politics*, New York, 1985.

J. Choper, *Judicial Review and the National Political Process*, Chicago, 1980.

J. Ely, *Democracy and Distrust: A Theory of Judicial Review*, Cambridge, Mass., 1980.

S. Halpern and C. Lamb (eds), *Judicial Activism and Restraint*, Lexington, 1982.

J. Rakove (ed.), *Interpreting the Constitution: the Debate Over Original Intent*, Boston, 1990.

B. Schwartz, *The New Right and the Constitution: Turning Back the Legal Clock*, Boston, 1990.

H. Wechsler, 'Towards Neutral Principles of Constitutional Law', *Harvard Law Review*, LXXVl, 1959, pp. 1–35.

C. Wolfe, *The Rise of Modern Judicial Review: From Constitutional Interpretation to Judge-Made Law*, New York, 1986.

Chapter Five—Supreme Court appointments

H. Abraham, *Justices and Presidents* (3rd edn), New York, 1992.

R. Bork, *The Tempting of America: The Political Seduction of the Law*, New York, 1990.

D. Brock, *The Real Anita Hill: The Untold Story*, New York, 1993.

E. Bronner, *Battle for Justice: How the Bork Nomination Shook America*, New York, 1989.

S. Carter, *The Confirmation Mess: Cleaning Up the Federal Appointments Process*, New York, 1994.

M. Gitenstein, *Matters of Principle: An Insider's Account of America's Rejection of Robert Bork's Nomination to the Supreme Court*, New York, 1992.

R. Hodder-Williams, 'The Strange Story of Judge Robert Bork and a Vacancy on the United States Supreme Court', *Political Studies*, XXXVI, 1988, pp. 613–37.

J. Mayer and J. Abramson, *Strange Justice: The Selling of Clarence Thomas*, New York, 1995.

R. McKeever, 'Courting the Congress: President Bush and the Nomination of David H. Souter', *Politics*, Xl, 1991, pp. 26–33.

M. Pertschuk and W. Schaetzel, *The People Rising: The Campaign Against the Bork Nomination*, New York, 1989.

H. Schwartz, *Packing the Courts: The Conservative Campaign to Rewrite the Constitution*, New York, 1988.

J. Simon, *In His Own Image: the Supreme Court in Richard Nixon's America*, New York, 1973.

P. Simon, *Advice and Consent*, Bethesda, Md., 1992.

L. Tribe, *God Save This Honorable Court: How the Choice of Supreme Court Justices Shapes Our History*, New York, 1985.

E. Witt, *A Different Justice: Reagan and the Supreme Court*, Washington, D.C., 1986.

Chapter Six—The power of the Supreme Court

T. Becker and M. Feeley, *The Impact of Supreme Court Decisions* (2nd edn), New York, 1973.

A. Bickel, *The Least Dangerous Branch*, Indianapolis, 1962.

L. Caplan, *The Tenth Justice*, New York, 1987.

C. Clayton, *The Politics of Justice: The Attorney General and the Making of Government Legal Policy*, Armonk, N.Y., 1992.

R. Davis, *Decisions and Images: The Supreme Court and the Press*, Englewood Cliffs, 1994.

L. Fisher, *Constitutional Dialogues: Interpretation As Political Process*, Princeton, 1988.

C. Fried, *Law and Order: Arguing the Reagan Revolution – A Firsthand Account*, New York, 1991.

C. Johnson and B. Canon, *Judicial Policies: Implementation and Impact*, Washington, D.C., 1984.

E. Keynes, *The Court vs. Congress: Prayer, Busing and Abortion*, Durham, N.C., 1989.

T. Marshall, *Public Opinion and the Supreme Court*, Boston, 1989.

W. Murphy, *Elements of Judicial Strategy*, Chicago, 1964.

K. O'Connor and L. Epstein, 'Amicus curiae participation in Supreme Court Litigation', *Law and Society*, XVI, 1981–2, pp. 311–20.

K. O'Connor and L. Epstein, 'Beyond Legislative Lobbying: Women's Rights groups and the Supreme Court', *Judicature*, LXVII, 1983, pp. 134–43.

G. Rosenberg, *The Hollow Hope: Can Courts Bring About Social Change*, Chicago, 1991.

R. Scigliano, *The Supreme Court and the Presidency*, New York, 1971.

Chapter Seven—The role of the Supreme Court in American government and politics

Many of the works listed above, especially in relation to Chapters Four and Six, are useful on this subject. But see also:

A. Cox, *The Role of the Supreme Court in American Government*, Oxford, 1976.

R. Dahl, 'Decision-Making in a Democracy: The Supreme Court as a National Policy-Maker', *Journal of Public Law*, VI, 1957, pp. 279–95: reprinted in M. Shapiro, *The Supreme Court and Public Policy*, Glenview, Ill., 1969, pp. 57–64.

W. Elliott, *The Rise of Guardian Democracy*, Cambridge, Mass., 1974.

N. Glazer, 'Toward an Imperial Judiciary', *The Public Interest*, XLI, 1975, pp. 104–23.

A. Miller, *The Supreme Court and American Capitalism*, New York, 1968.

A. Miller, *Toward Increased Judicial Activism: The Political Role of the Supreme Court*, Westport, Conn., 1982.

Case index

Most of the references below relate to the US Supreme Court Reports. With some recent cases, however, reference is made to the Lawyers Edition of the Reports, the Supreme Court Reporter or simply the case Docket Number.

General index